Dave Thomas
A Decade of Dave in Advertising

**Photography by
Robert Levite**

Photography © Robert Levite, 1999

All rights reserved. No part of this work covered by copyrights hereon may be reproduced or used in any form or by any means—graphic, electronic or mechanical, including photocopying, recording, taping of information on storage or retrieval systems—without the prior written permission of the publisher.

The copyright on each photograph in this book belongs to the photographer, and no reproductions of the photographic images contained herein may be made without the express permission of the photographer.

Art Direction – Paul Kreft
Cover, Book Design, and Project Management – Kevin Pease
Copywriting – Robert Levite, Garry Bergman, Don Calhoon

Millennium Marketing
827A Eastgate South Drive
Cincinnati, Ohio 45245

Publisher's Cataloging-in-Publication
Levite, Robert.
   Dave Thomas : a decade of Dave in advertising/photographs by Robert Levite. -- 1st ed.
   p. cm.
   ISBN 0-9659352-8-0

   1. Wendy's International--In mass media.
   2. Advertising campaigns--United States.
   3. Thomas, R. David, 1932--Pictoral works.
   4. Restauranteurs--United States--Pictoral works.
   I. Title.

HF6169.W46L48 1999   659.113'0973
                       QBI99-1403

Printed in Hong Kong

The Saga Begins

In early 1989, Wendy's Marketing Department met with its agency, Bates USA, in a conference room in New York City. Dave Thomas, Founder of Wendy's International and Chairman of the Board, shared his wisdom and passion for a business he had loved most of his life. It was this passion that led to the suggestion Mr. Thomas appear in the advertising. After much prodding, a commercial was shot and a legend was born.

Ten years and 652 commercials later, Mr. Thomas has become "Dave," an American icon. And the advertising campaign has flourished. Throughout its history it has won numerous advertising and marketing awards and even earned Dave a place in the *Guinness Book of World Records* for "Longest Running TV Campaign Featuring A Company Founder."

How does a campaign become so successful? Promises made are kept. To that end, the Wendy's System might just be the real hero. Dave's promise of a quality product at a good price is delivered on a daily basis. The System's enthusiasm has been an inspiration to Mr. Thomas, and while he has maintained an ability to laugh at himself, he remains in awe of people who are dedicated to excellence.

Obviously this book portrays only a sampling of the many commercials produced. But it serves as a tribute to one very special man and the hundreds of people working countless hours who, through their dedication, have built the most successful and enduring advertising campaign in the history of the restaurant business.

"I can't believe I've been doing this for ten years!"

In 1989, the campaign took flight.

From old cars to old hats, Dave looks classic
in whatever we put him in.

Nice tie.

Believe it or not,
it's no vacation making commercials.

Dave turns the tables on Director
of Photography, Sal Guida.

Dave enjoys visits from franchisees like Mike Toukan,
who want to see how commercials are made.

Dave sells pitas on a Hollywood set,
built in Florida.

"Aren't you a little dressed up for a diner, Mr. Thomas?"

"This is the only thing they'll let me wear."

"Hail, Caesar!" (Salad?)

Every family has a cousin Ed.

Dave finishes a commercial that started in New Jersey
and ended in San Francisco.
Four days of work for thirty seconds of film.

"Action!"

With Kristi Yamaguchi.

With Ben Stein.

With you know who.

Dave looks for a bus stop after giving
his car away in a Super Value Menu spot.

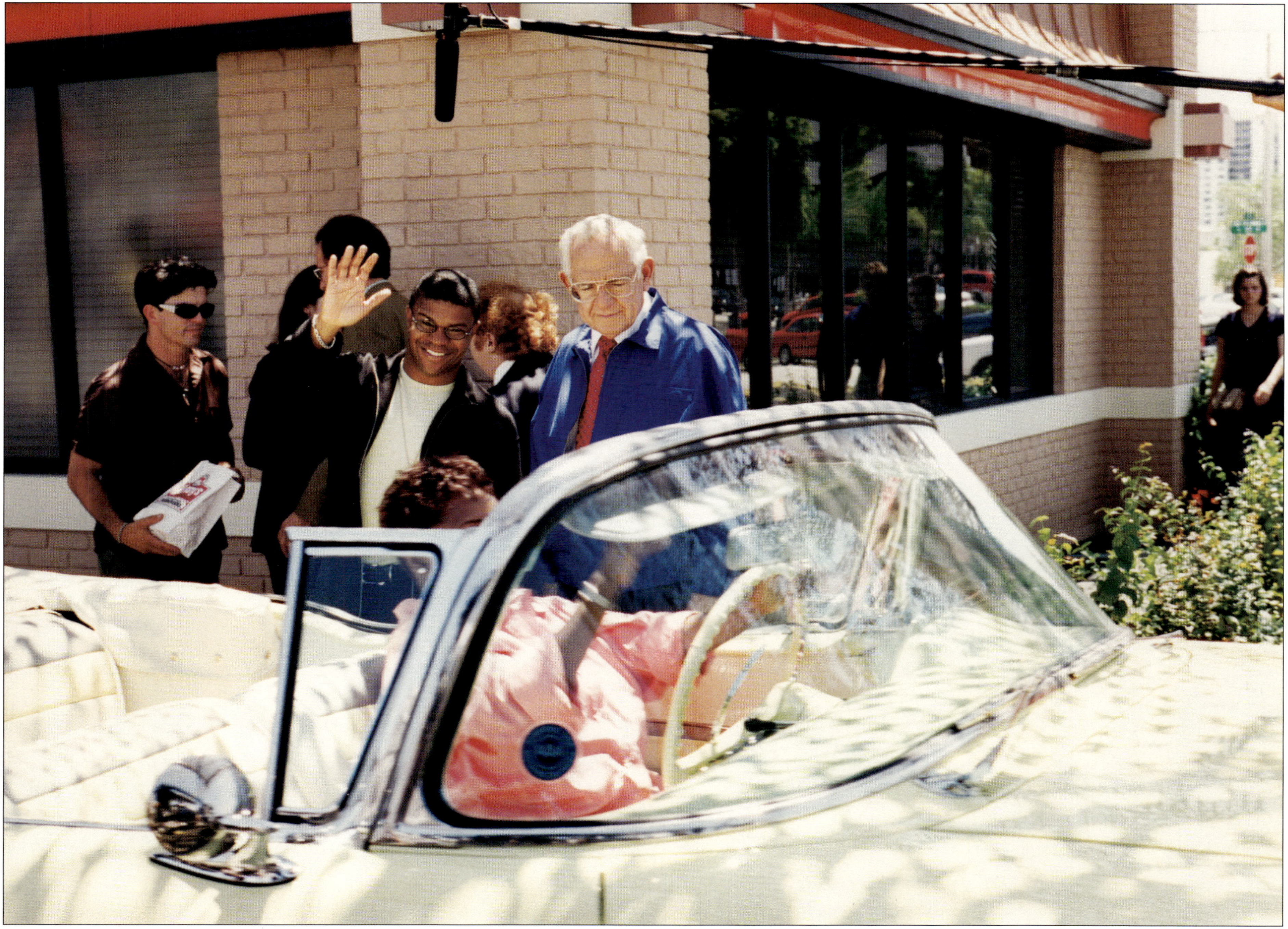

"I'm ready for my close-up, Mr. Hudson."
(Bill Hudson has directed Dave's spots for 10 years.)

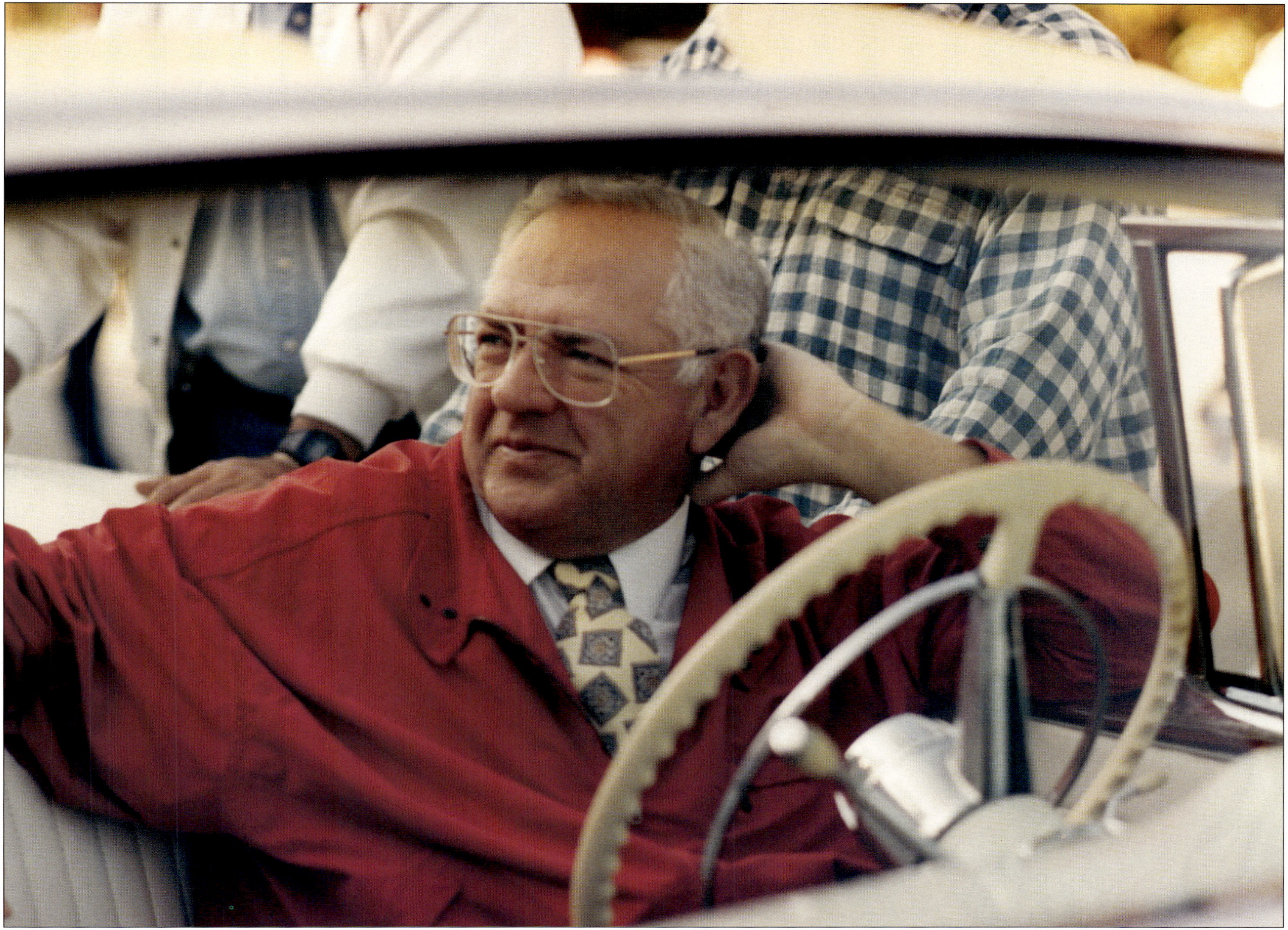

"Take this to 498 Seventh Avenue."

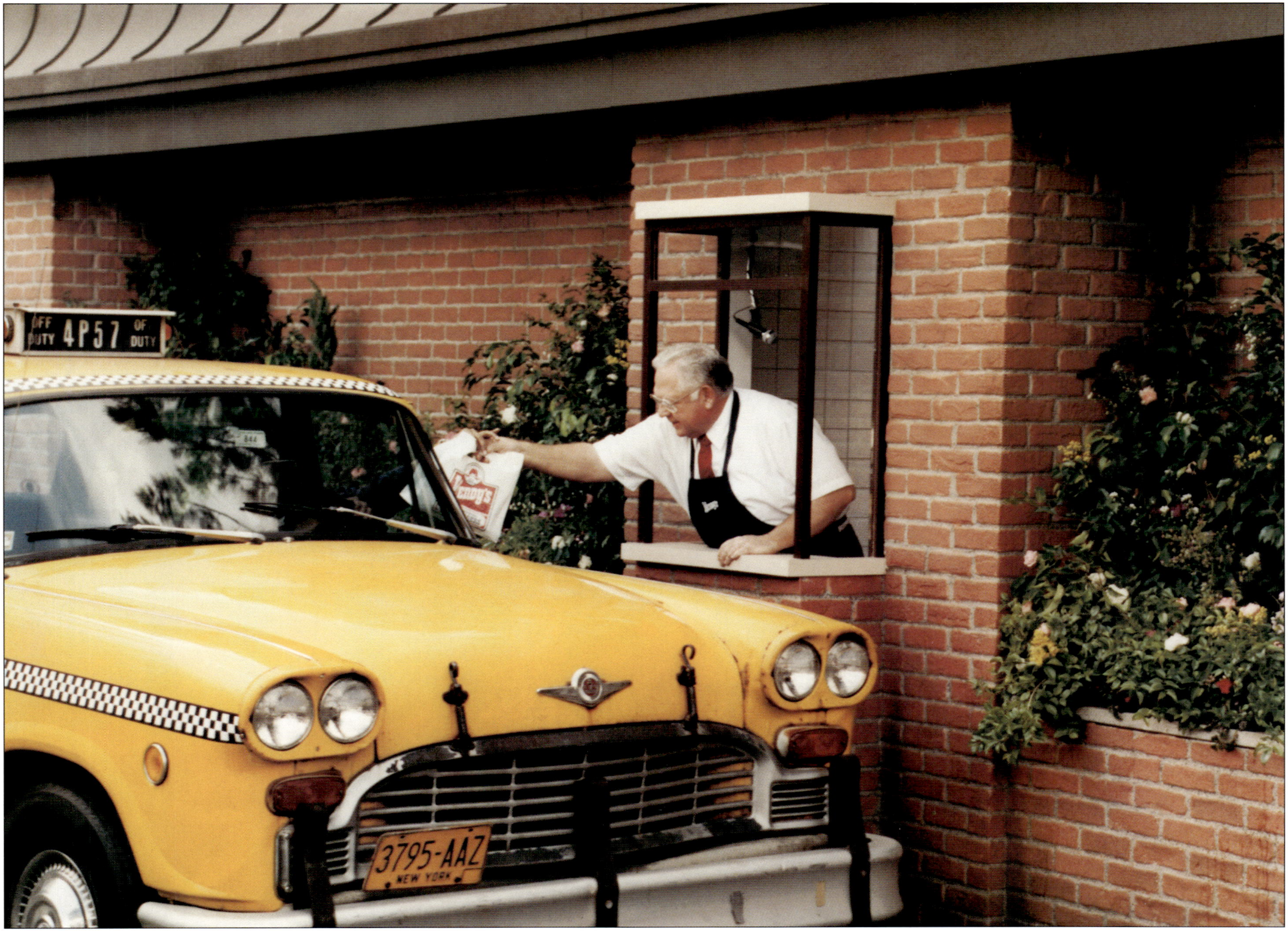
4P57
3795-AAZ
NEW YORK

"But officer, the fries were getting cold."

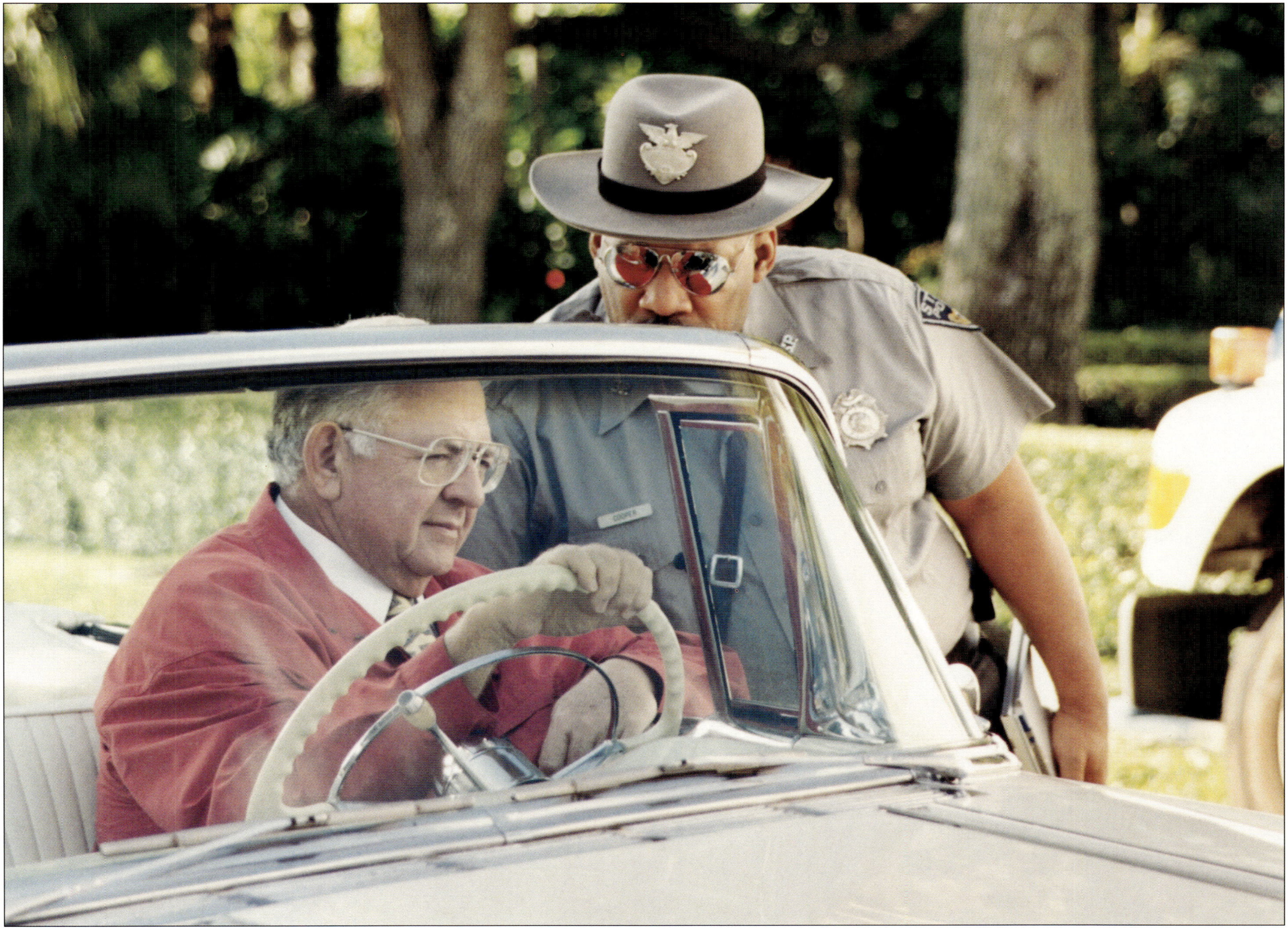

"Lorraine won't let me keep it."

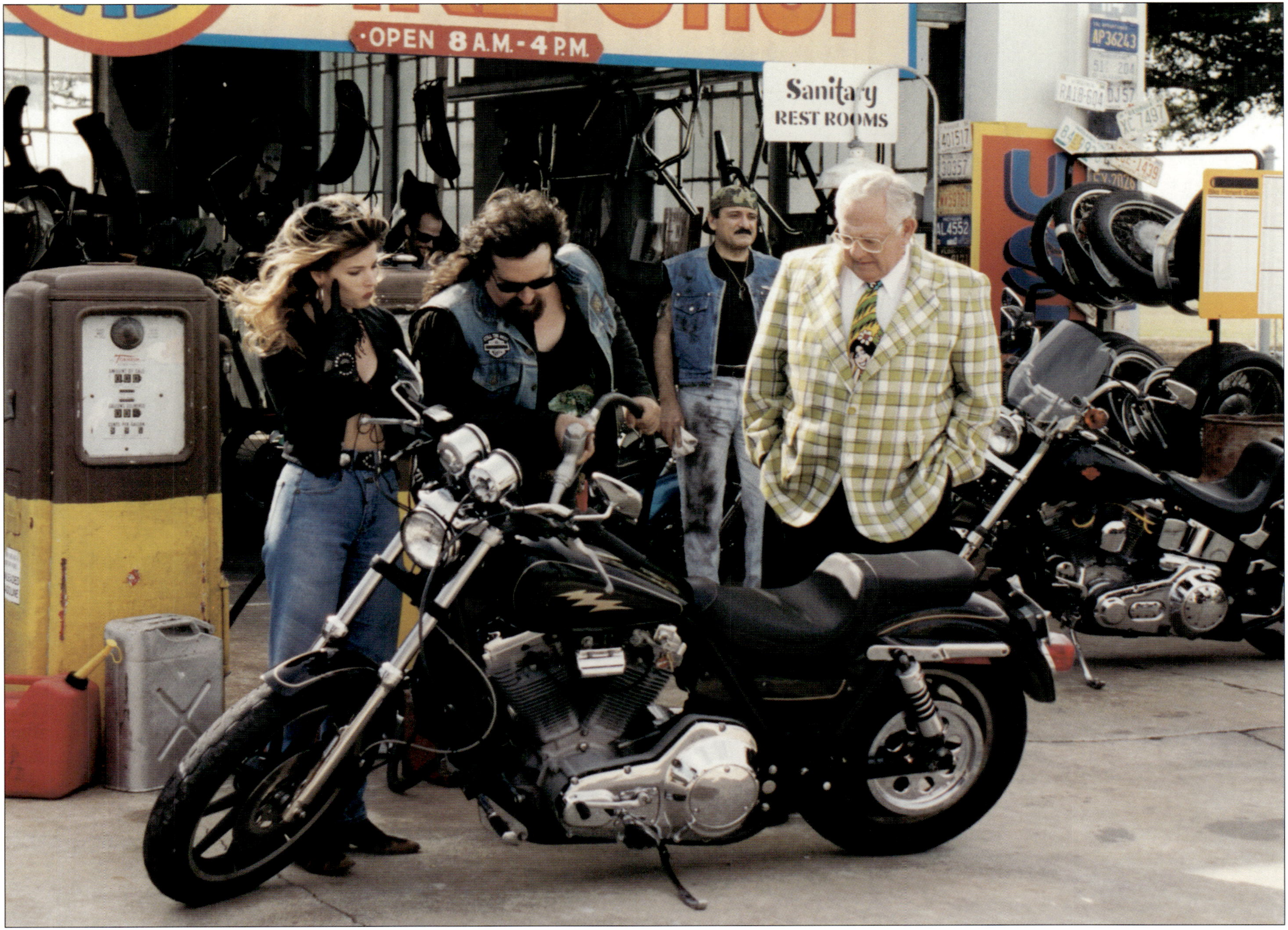

OPEN 8 A.M.-4 P.M.
Sanitary
REST ROOMS

Regardless of the situation...

...Dave's message is always clear.

"If Dave were here, I'd give him a big hug."

"He'll be sorry he missed you."

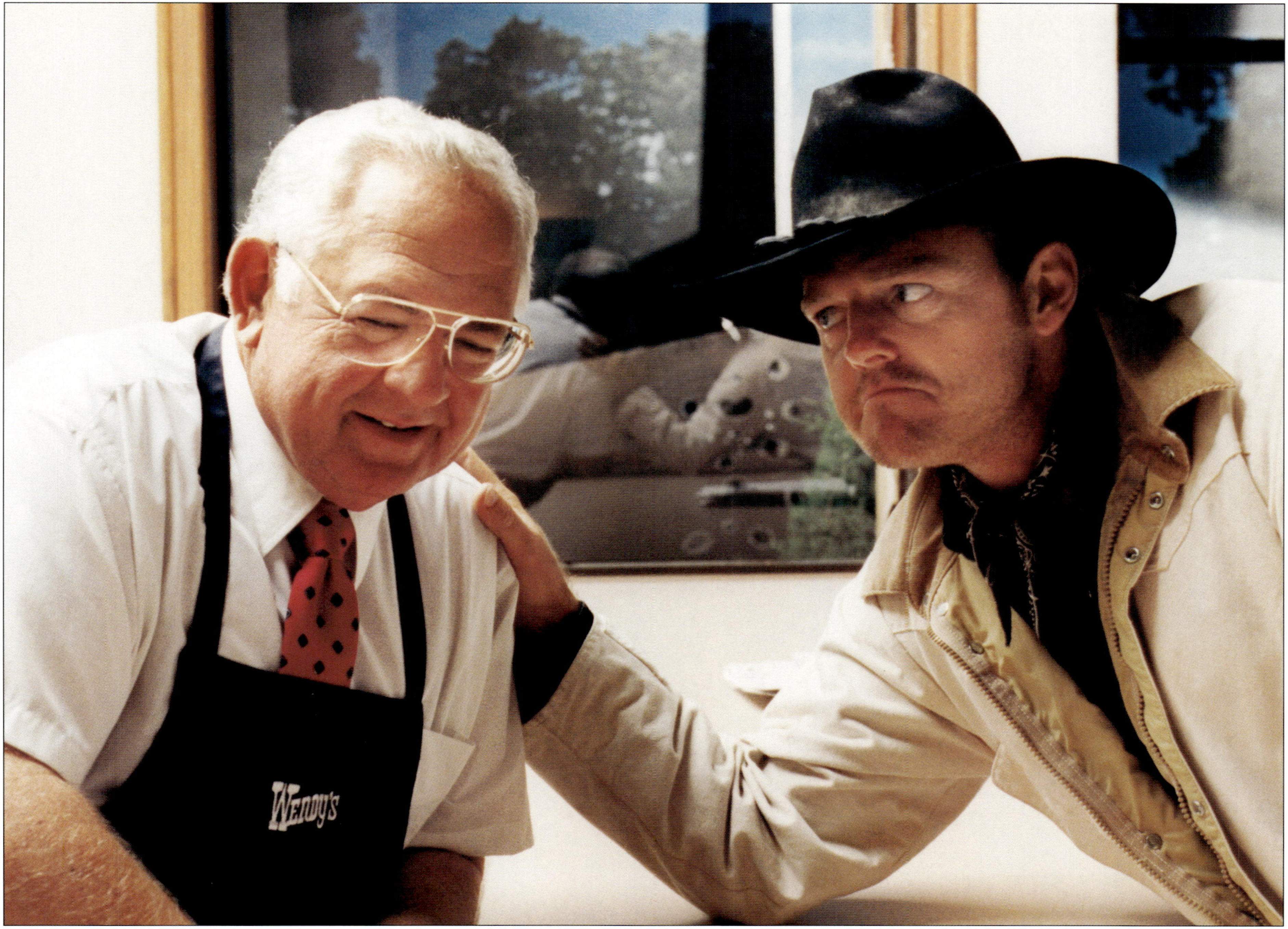
Wendy's

"This is lighter than it looks."

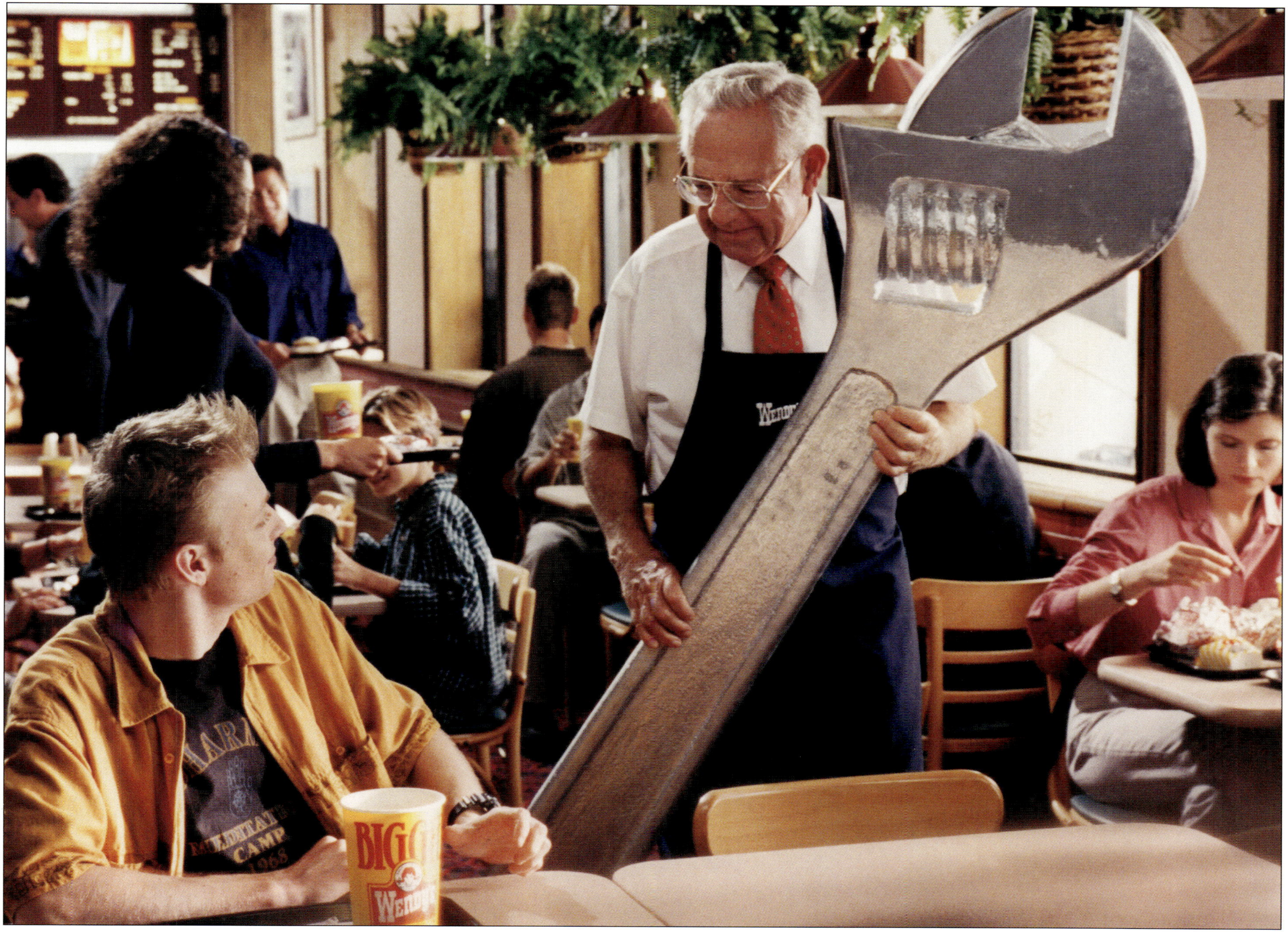
BIG

Dave in the heat of competition.
"How much are we playing for?"

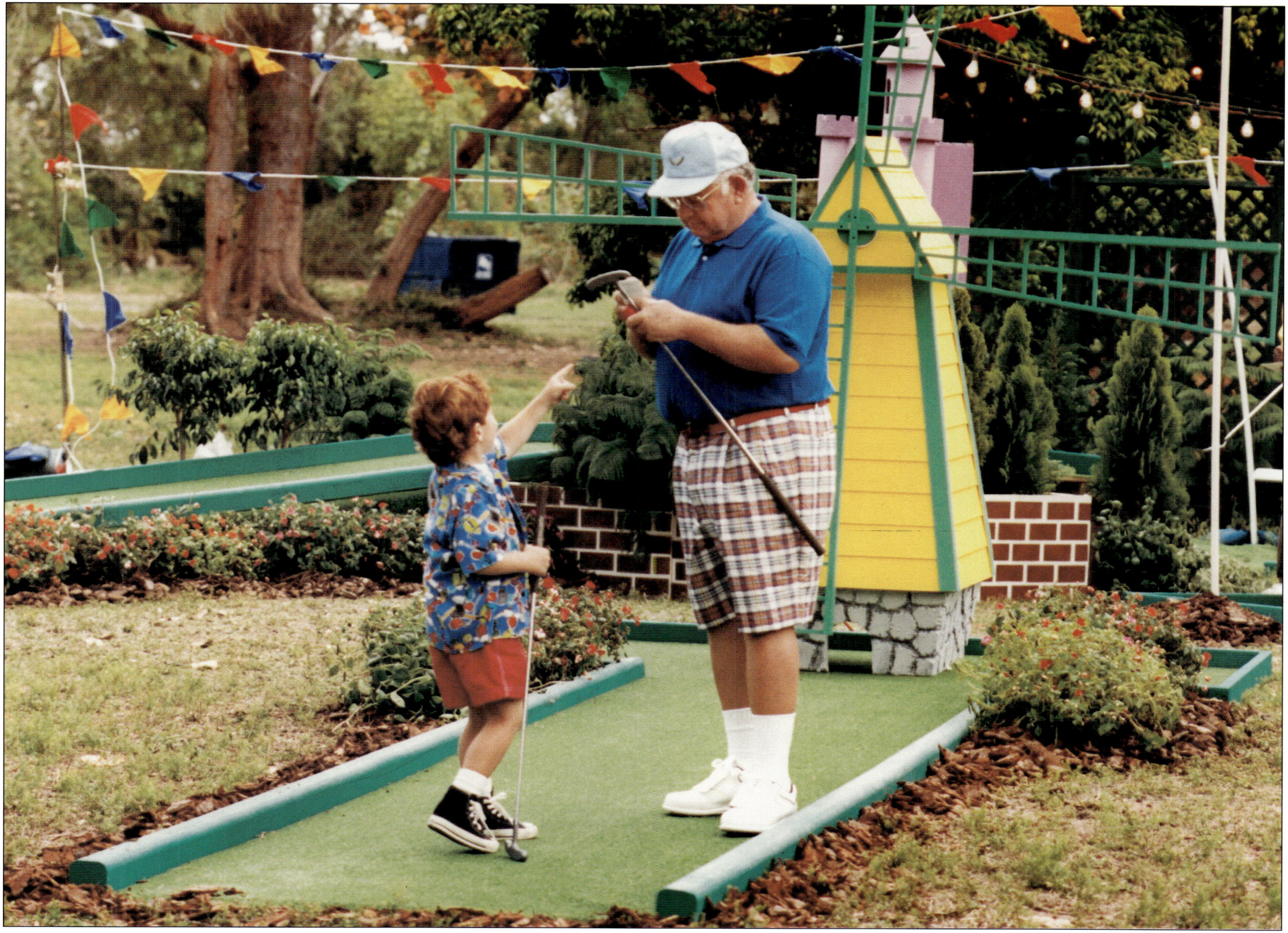

Serenading Dave, the late character actor
Skip Chertoff appeared in over 126 commercials.

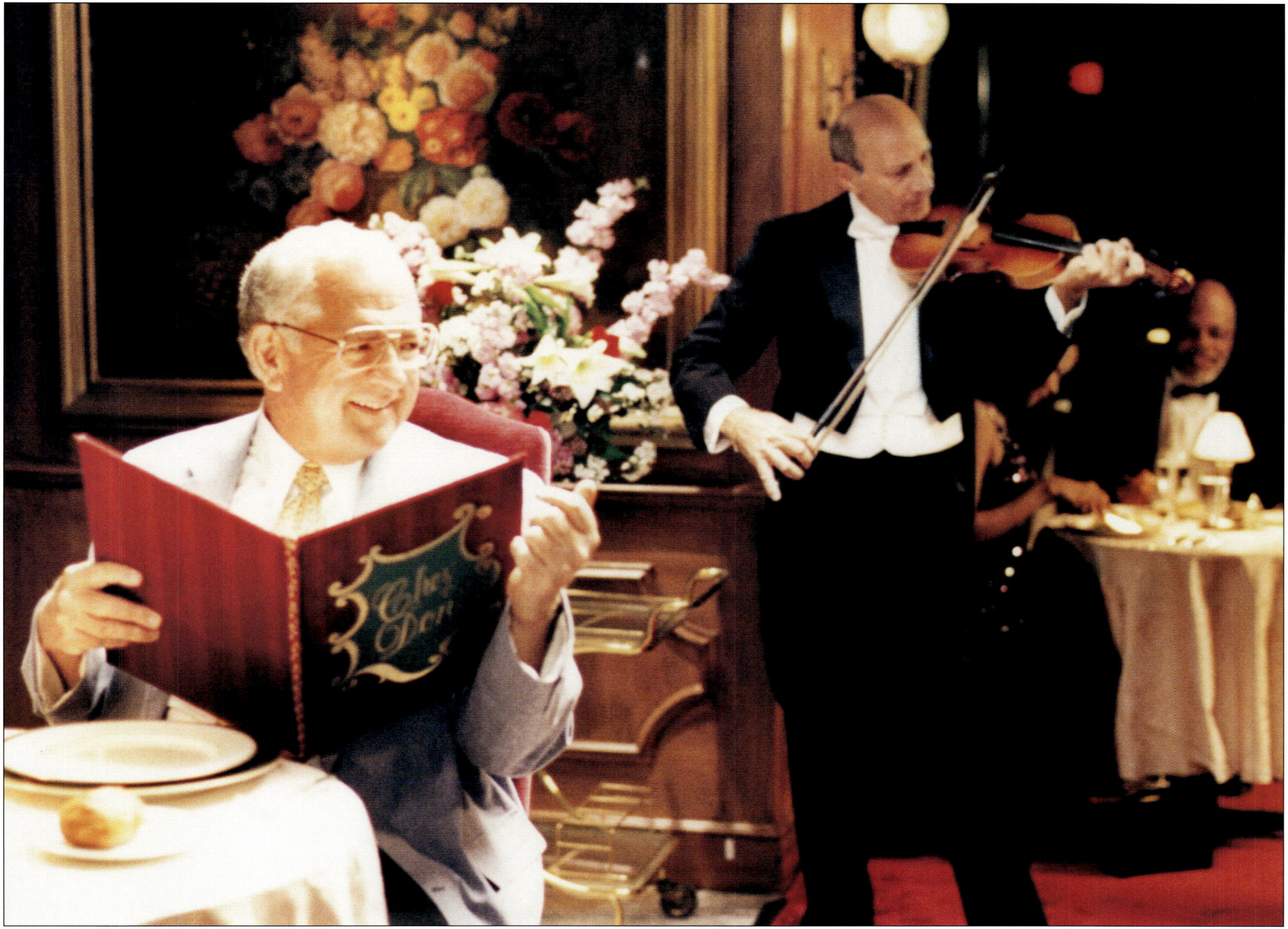

The white shirt and red tie
were at the cleaners.

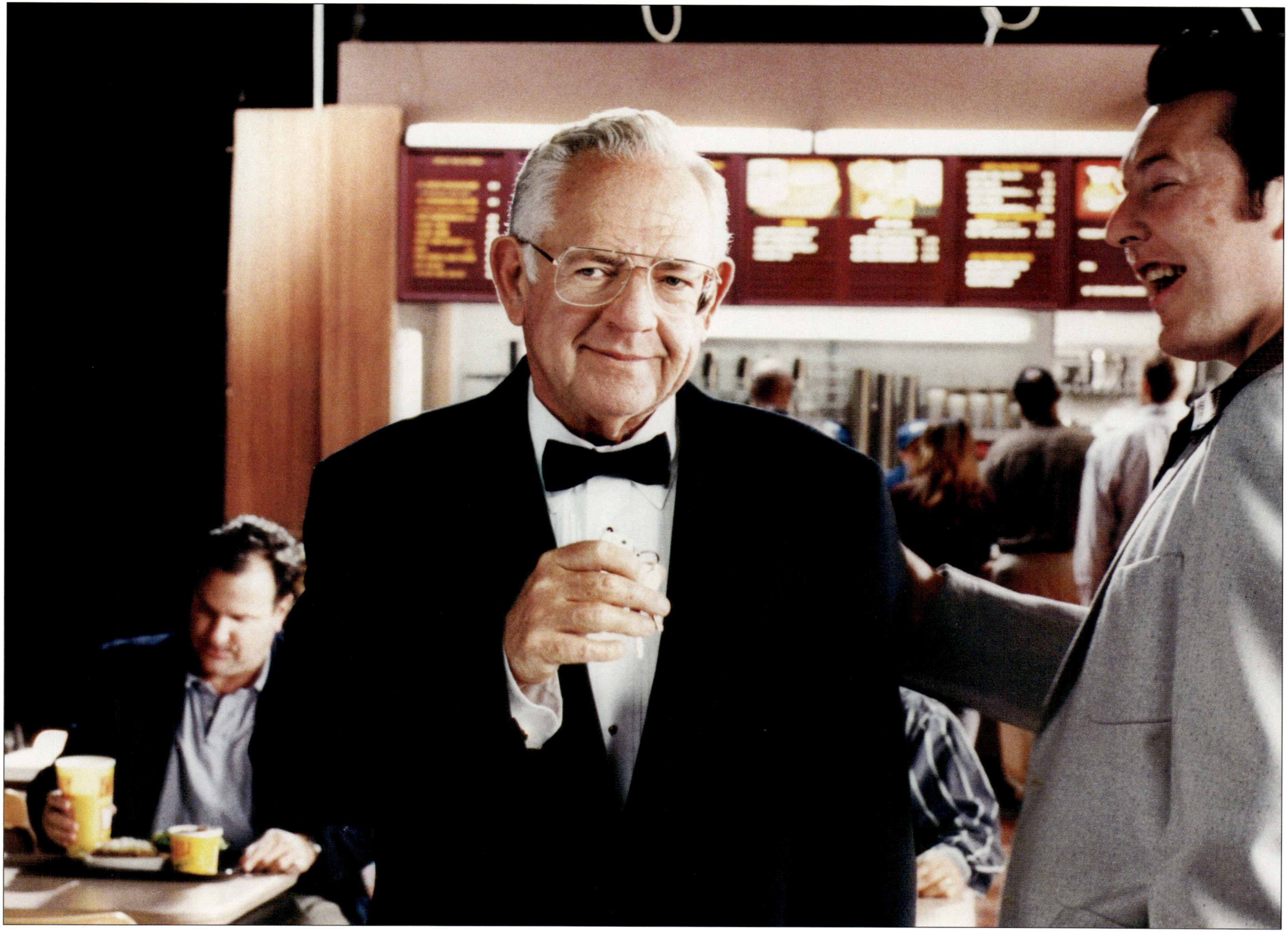

"What was my line?"

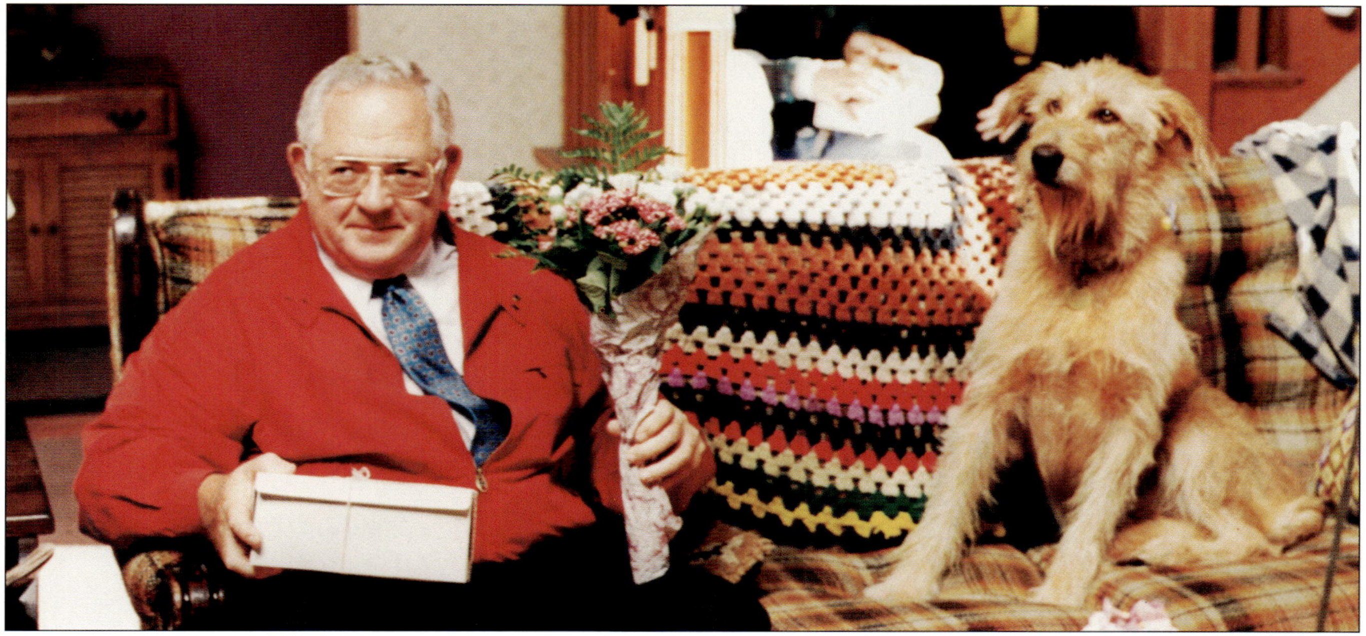

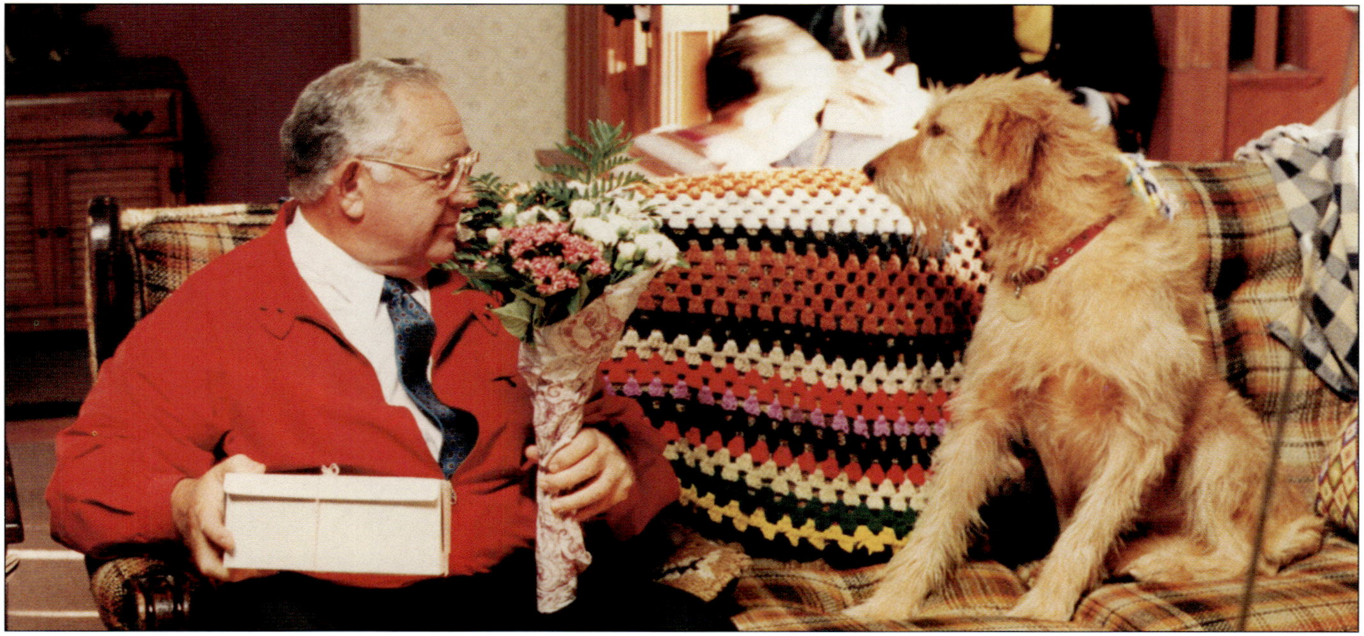

Working in snow in August
to get ready for Winter Olympics advertising.

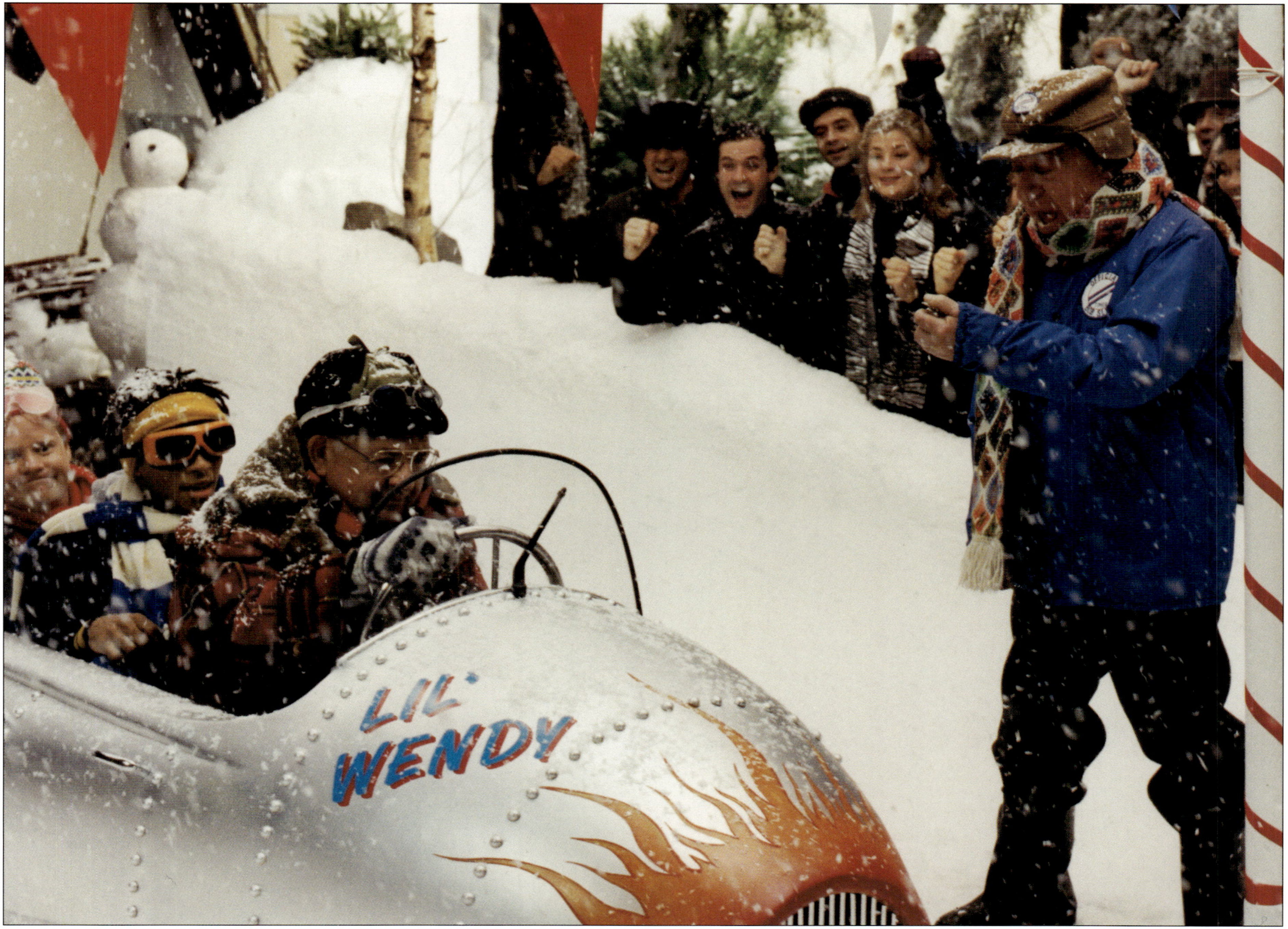
LIL'
WENDY

"...It's called Wendy's...We serve hamburgers..."

SMOKE
HOUSE
TEXAS 56
FP6815
172-55
24-320
RHODE ISLAND
UK-717
1949 - OHIO
Charlies Specials
SMOKED CHEESES
Chedder Gouda
Munster
ROYAL CROWN COLA

On location in San Francisco—

"Please don't make me walk up that hill again."

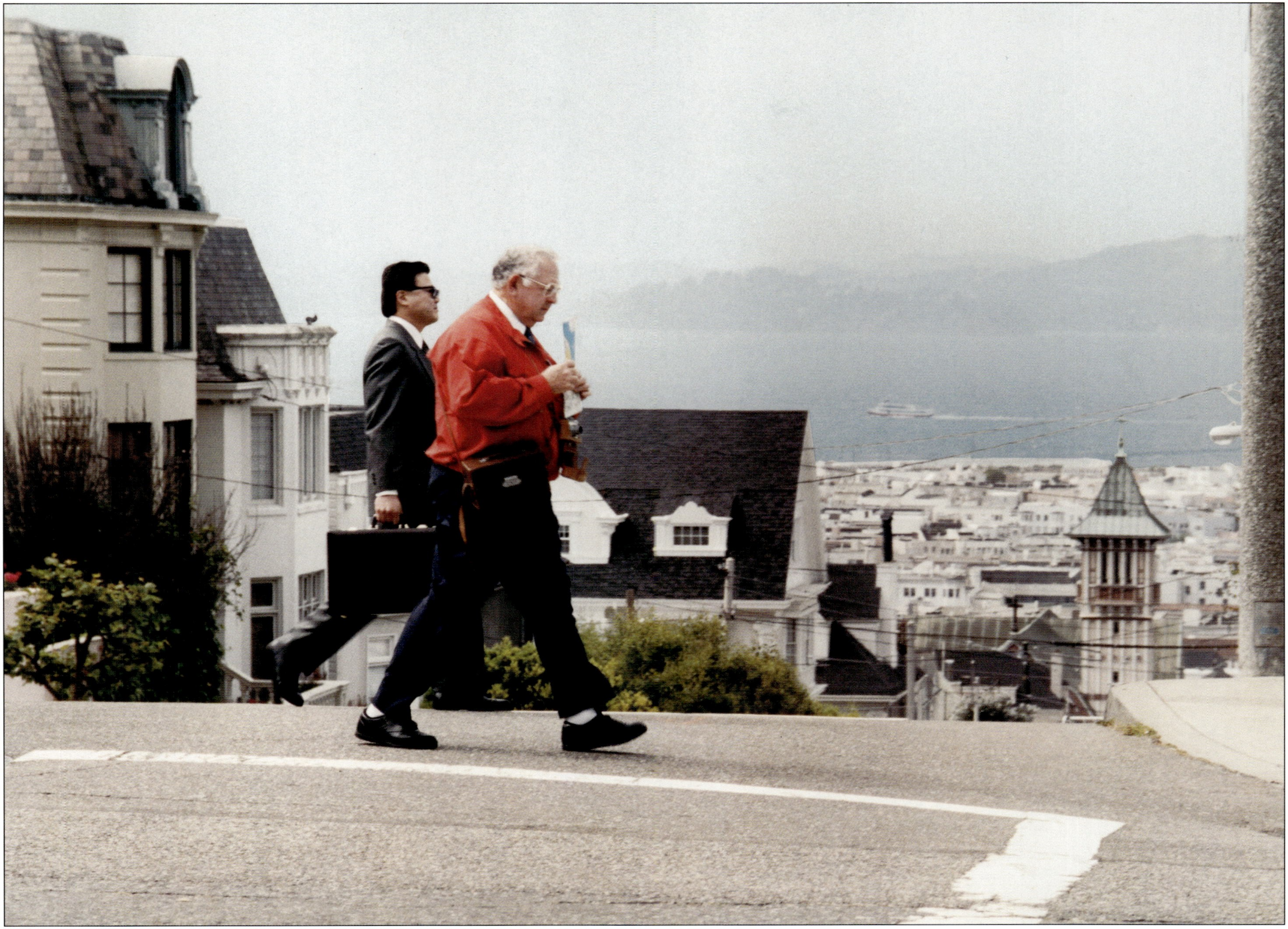

Nice carrots. Strange farmer.

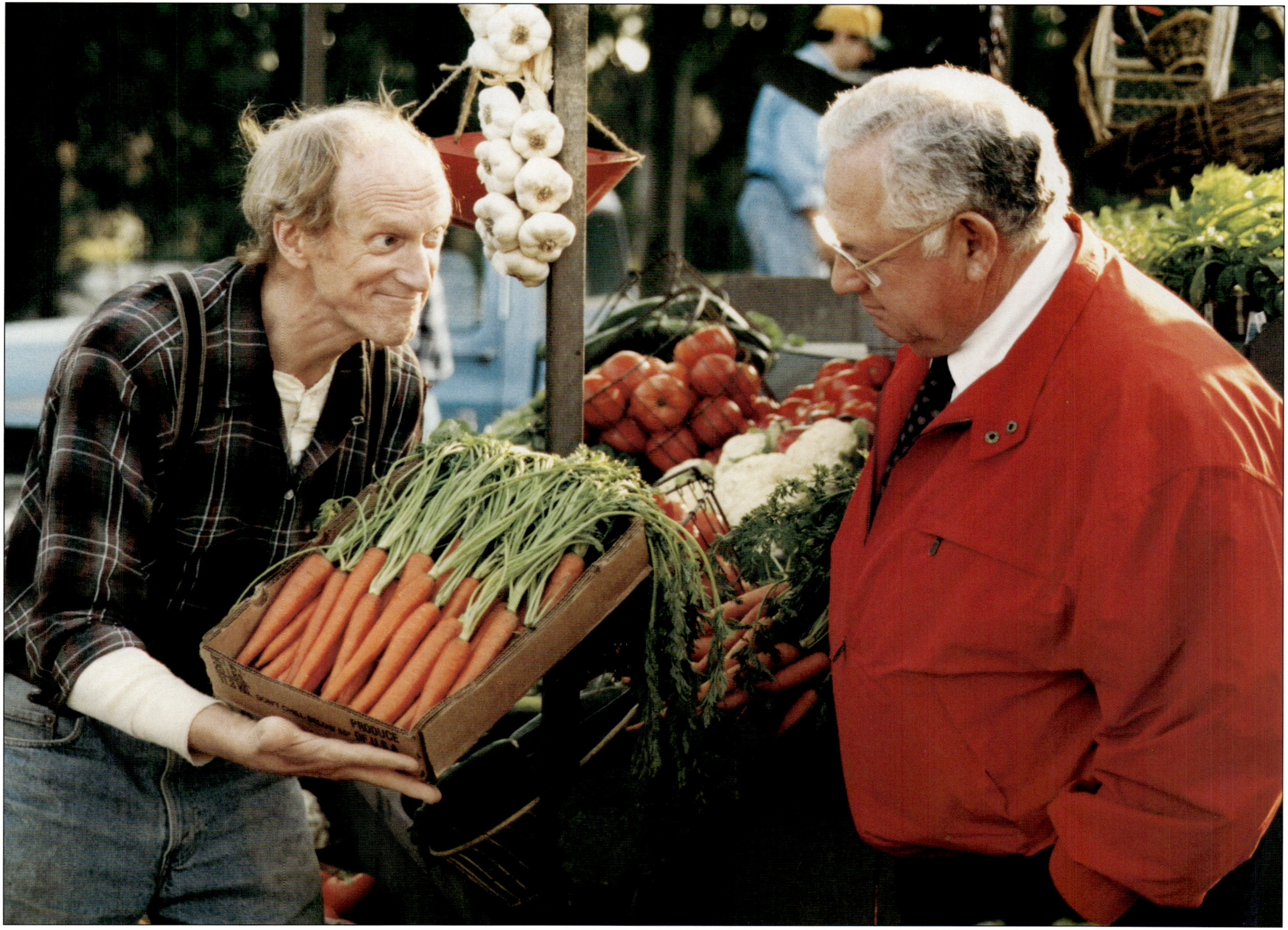
PRODUCE

Dave Rocks.

Dave Rocks HARD.

With chicken nuggets, you can run
but you can't hide.

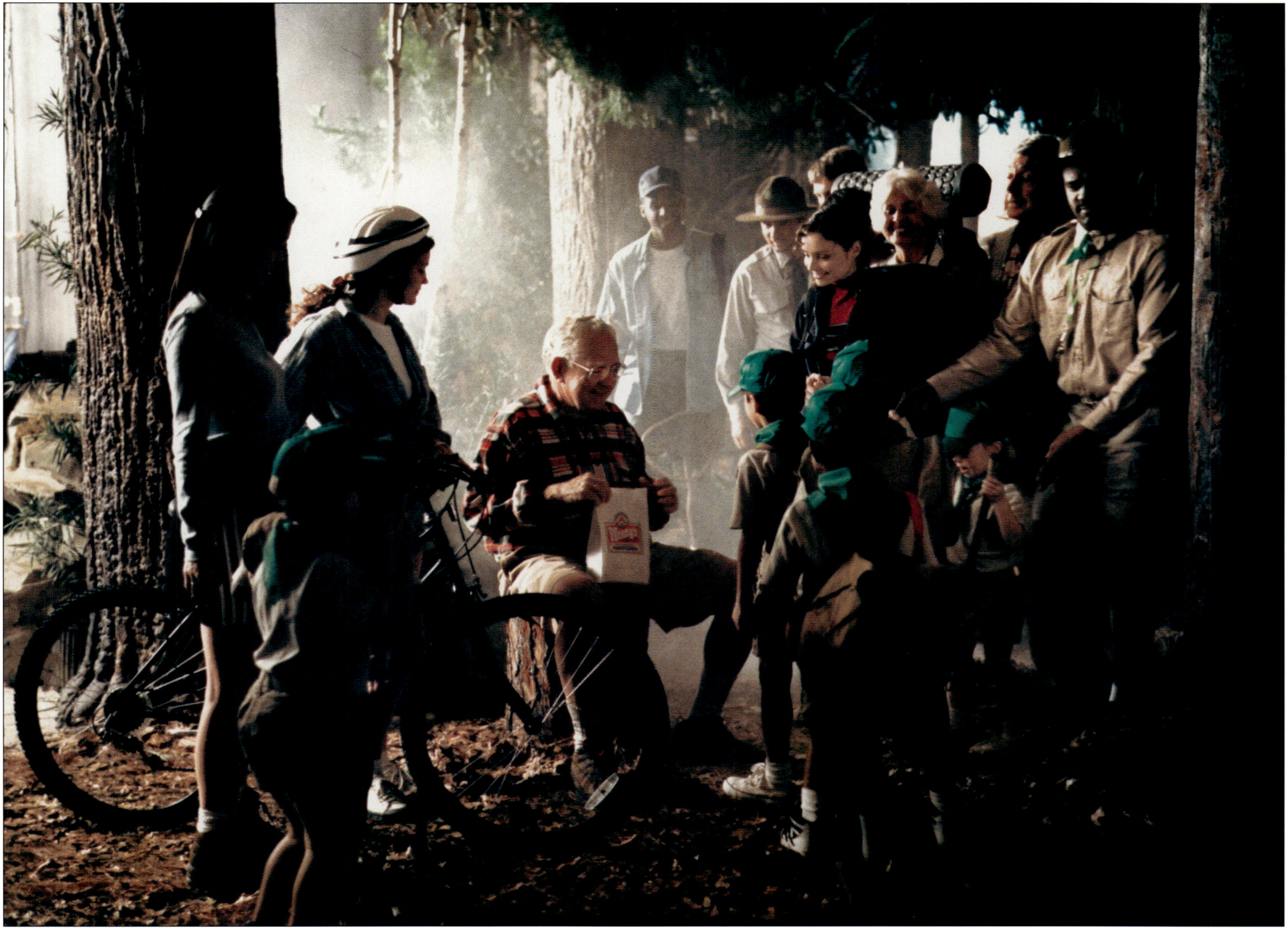

Everyone loves a parade—
Dave enjoys one of five parades staged over the past 10 years.

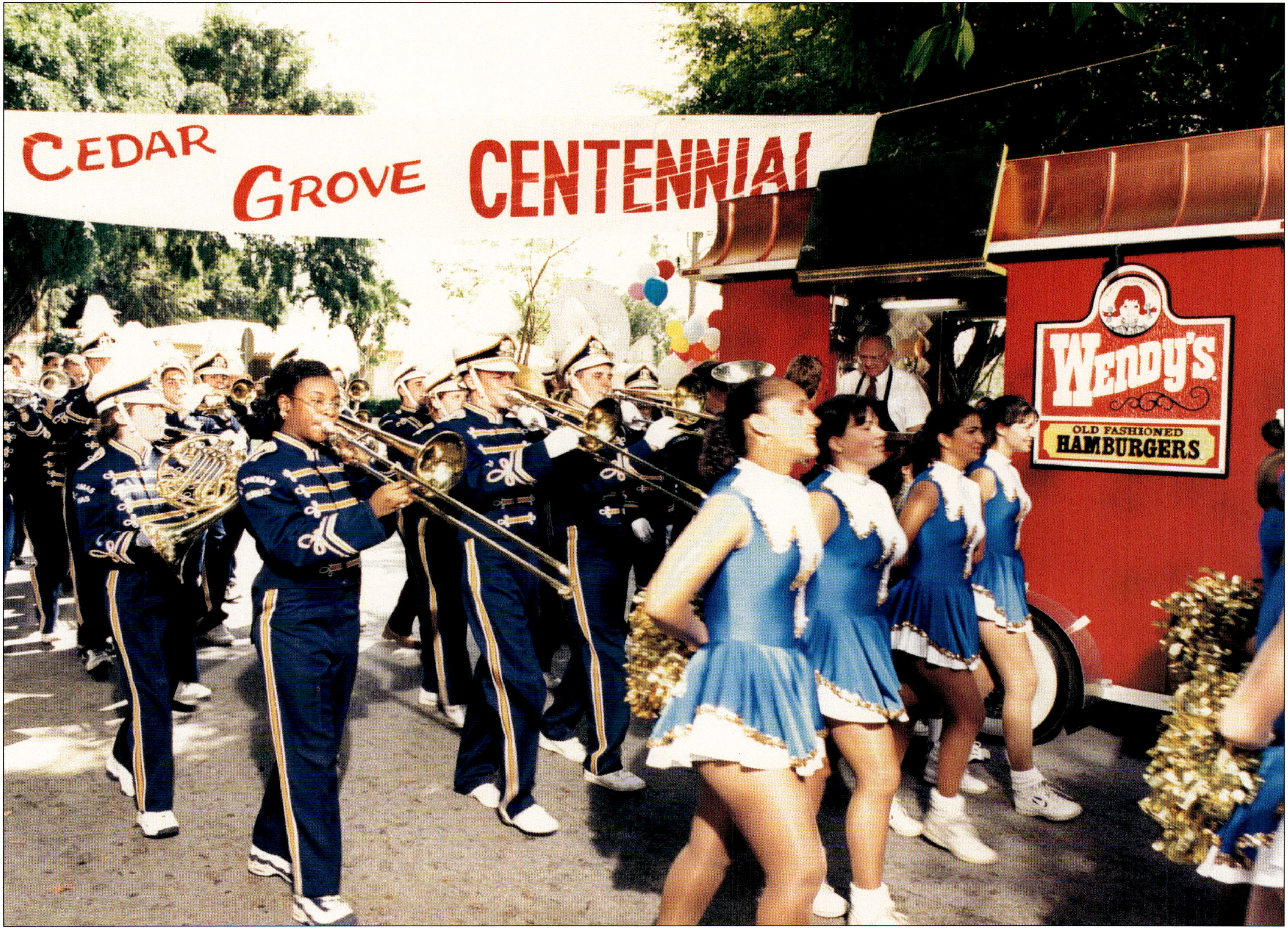
CEDAR GROVE CENTENNIAL
WENDY'S
OLD FASHIONED
HAMBURGERS

Friends can always count on Dave to bring the food.

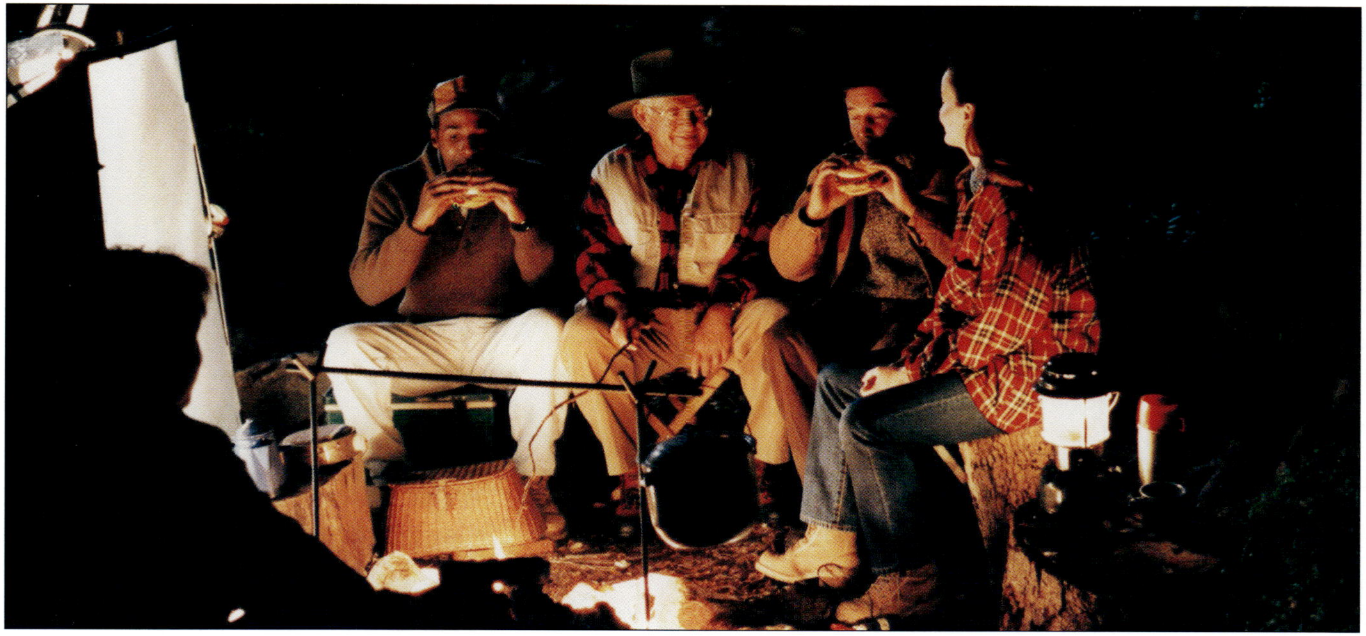

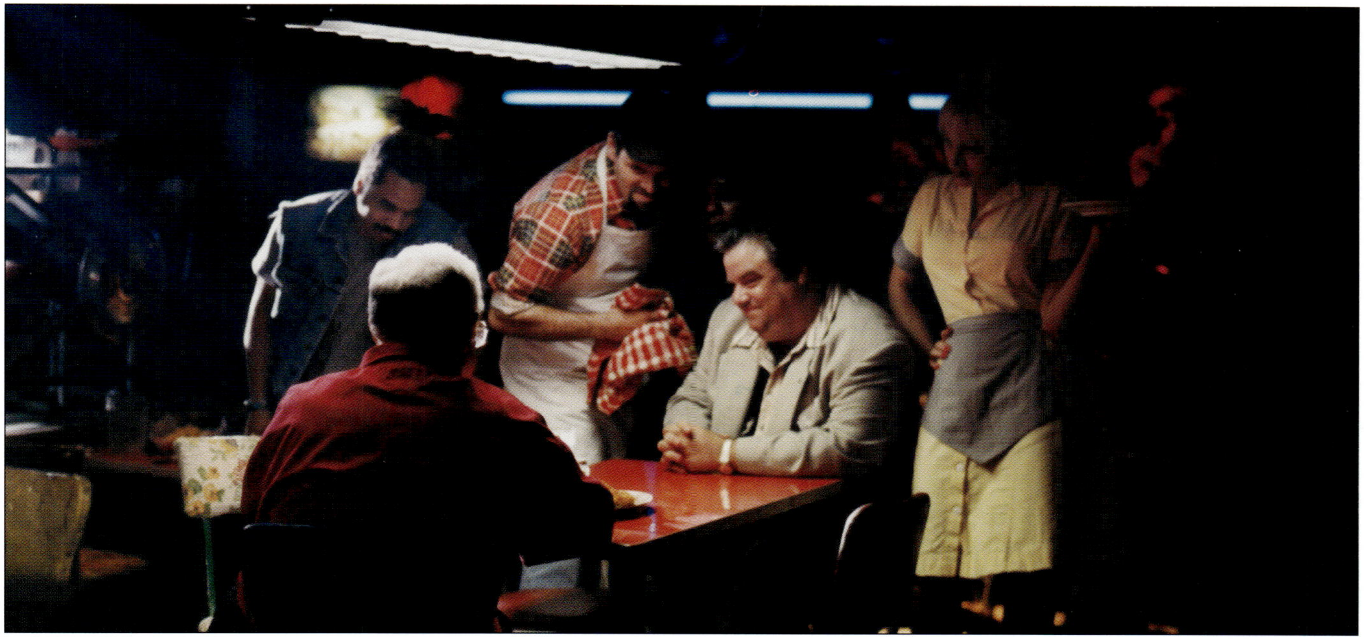

"It's just what I wanted!
How did you know?"

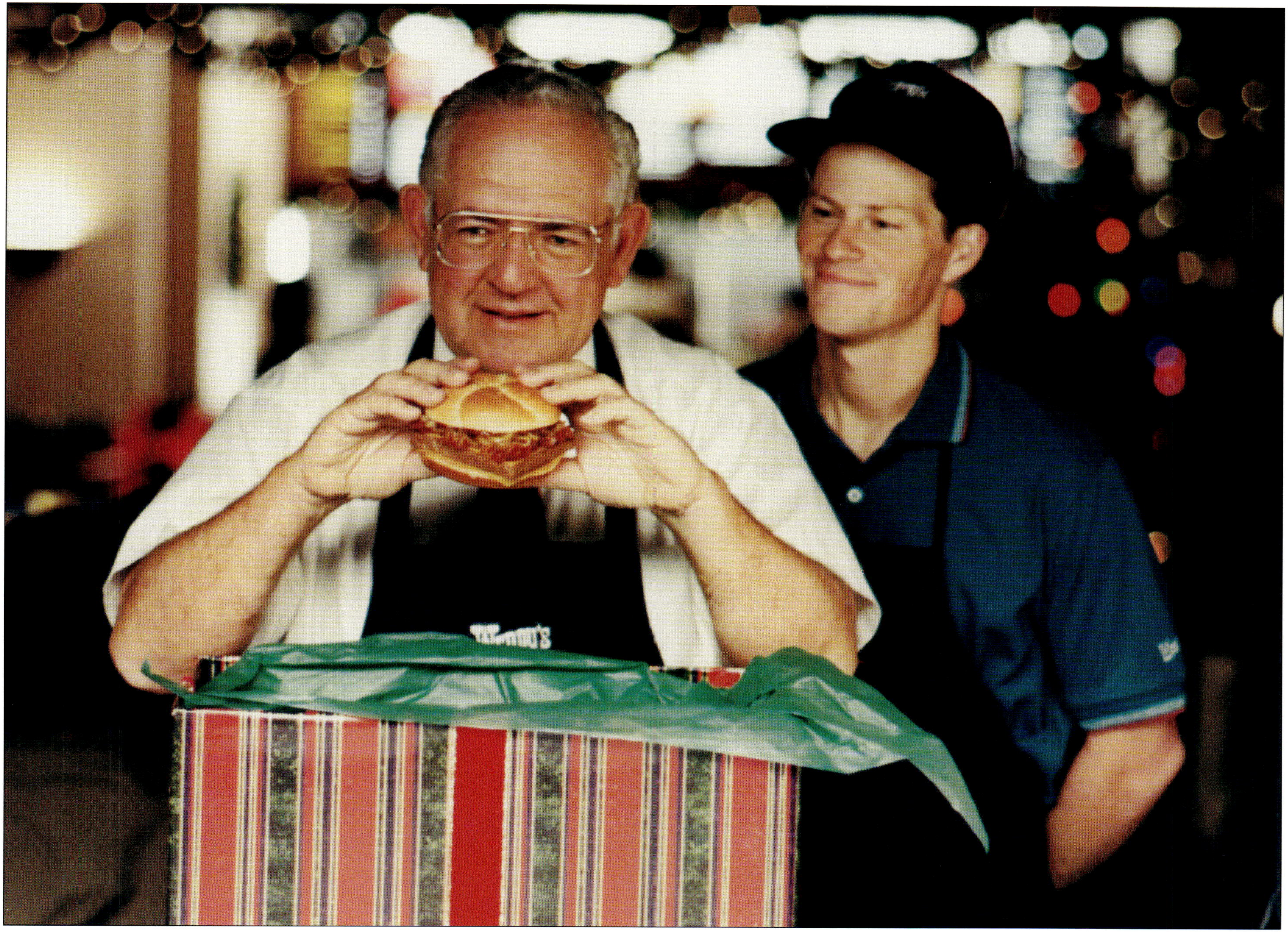

"Dear Dave..."

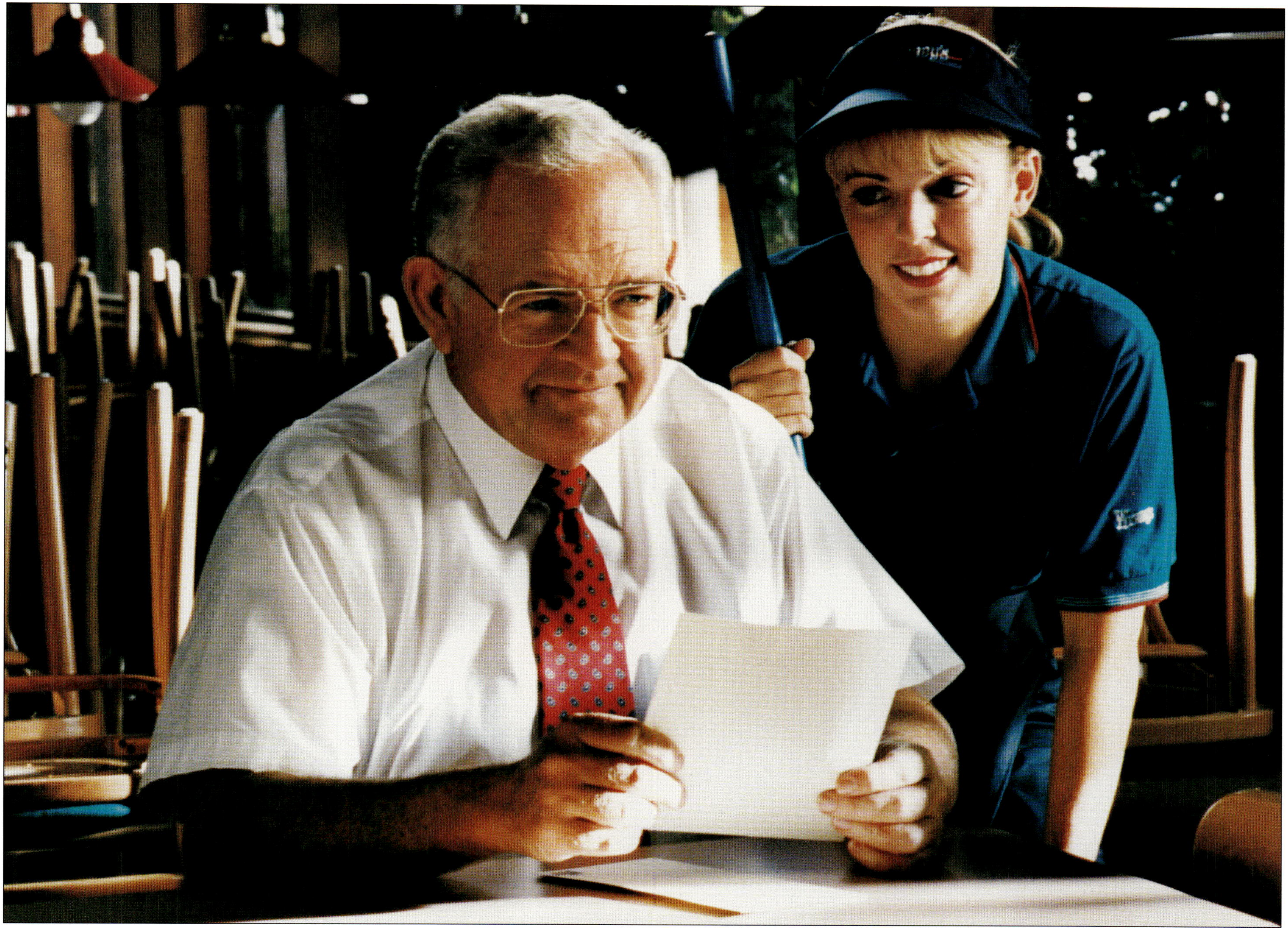

The Big Eaters Club comes to order...
and the order was Big Bacon Classic Combos.

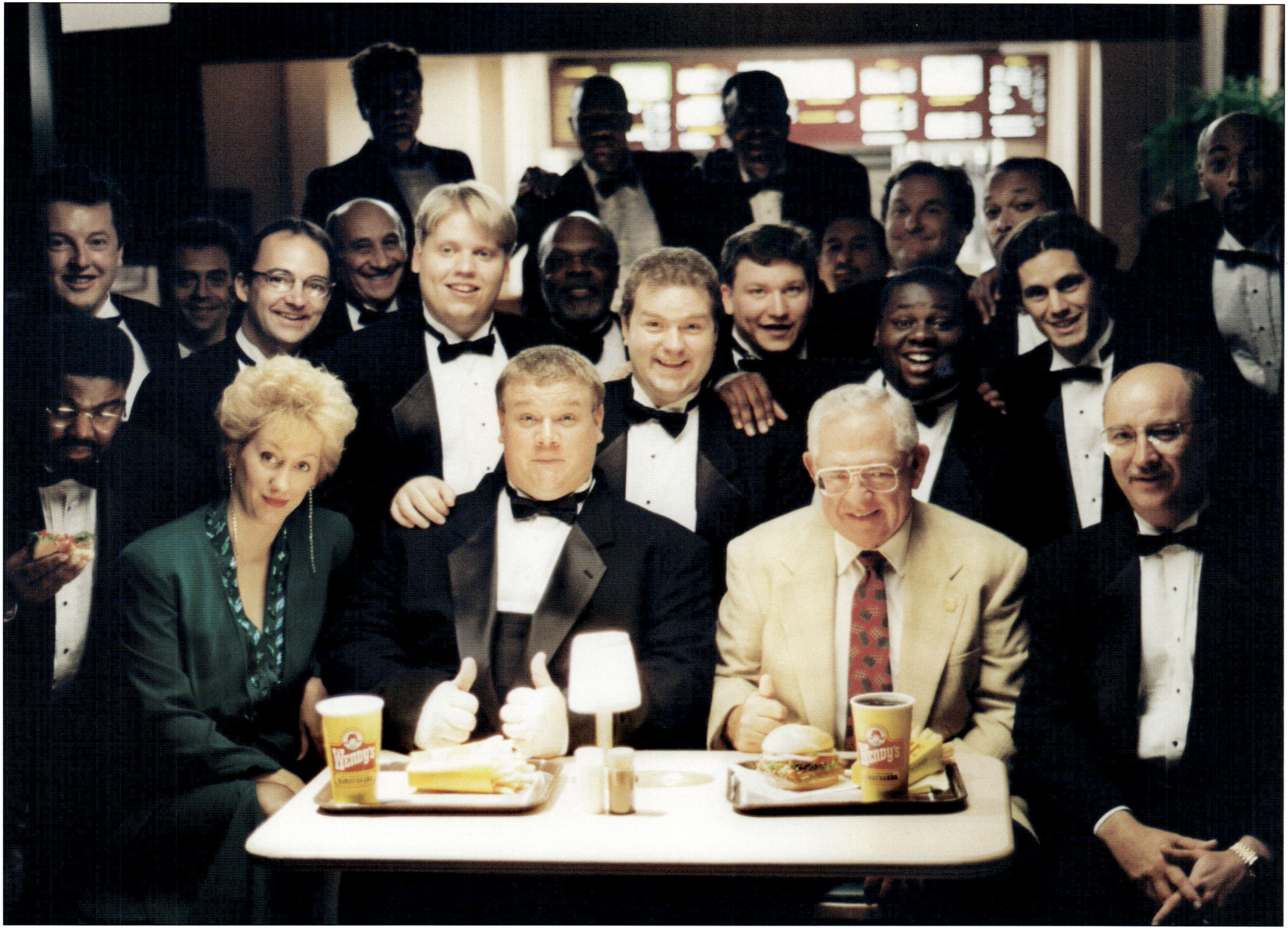

Wendy's
Wendy's

Never enough of a good thing

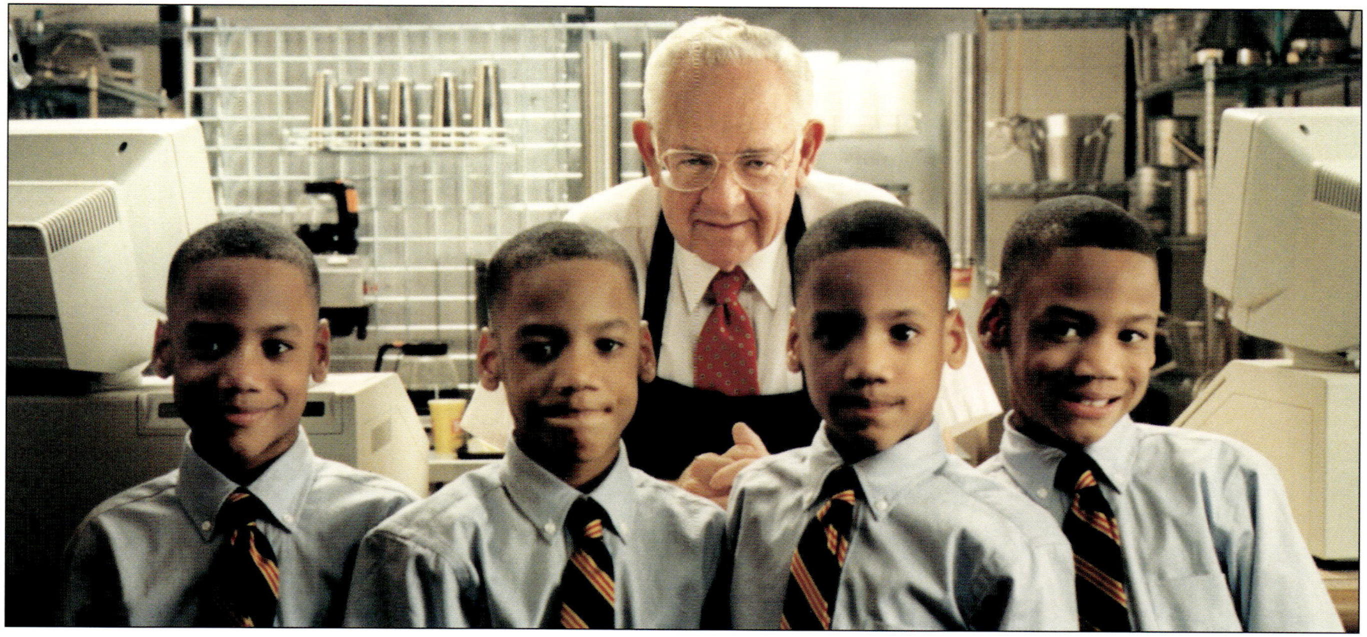

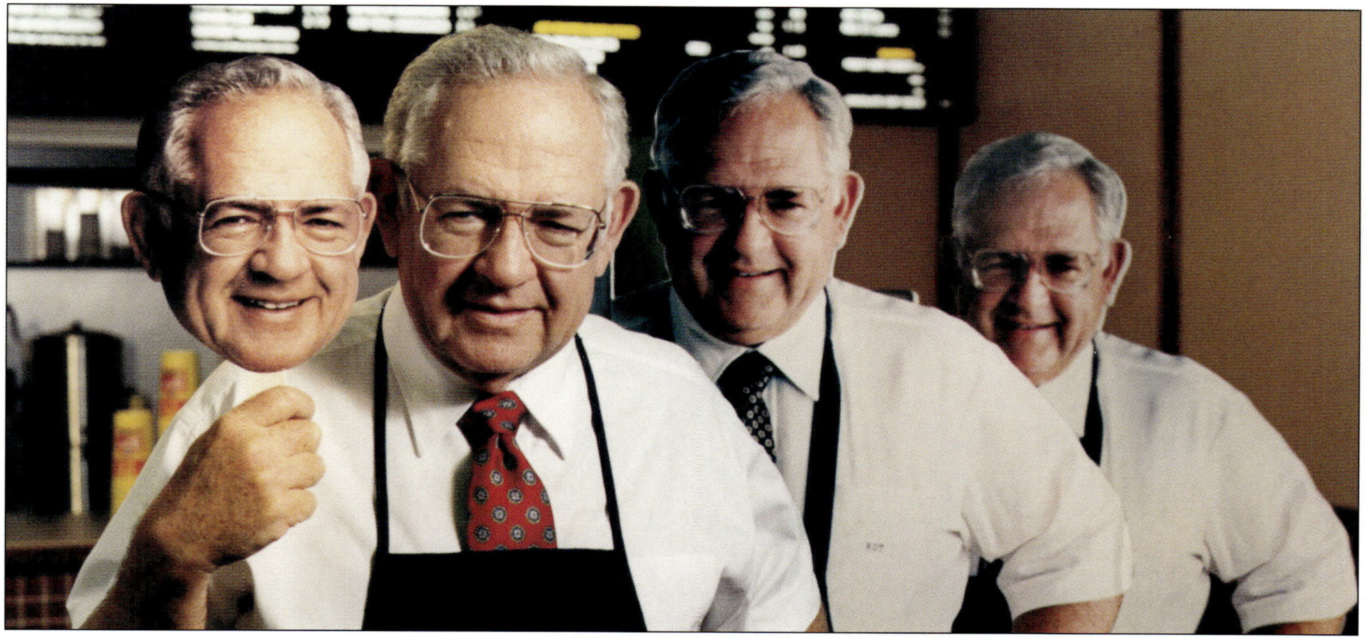

Bingo!

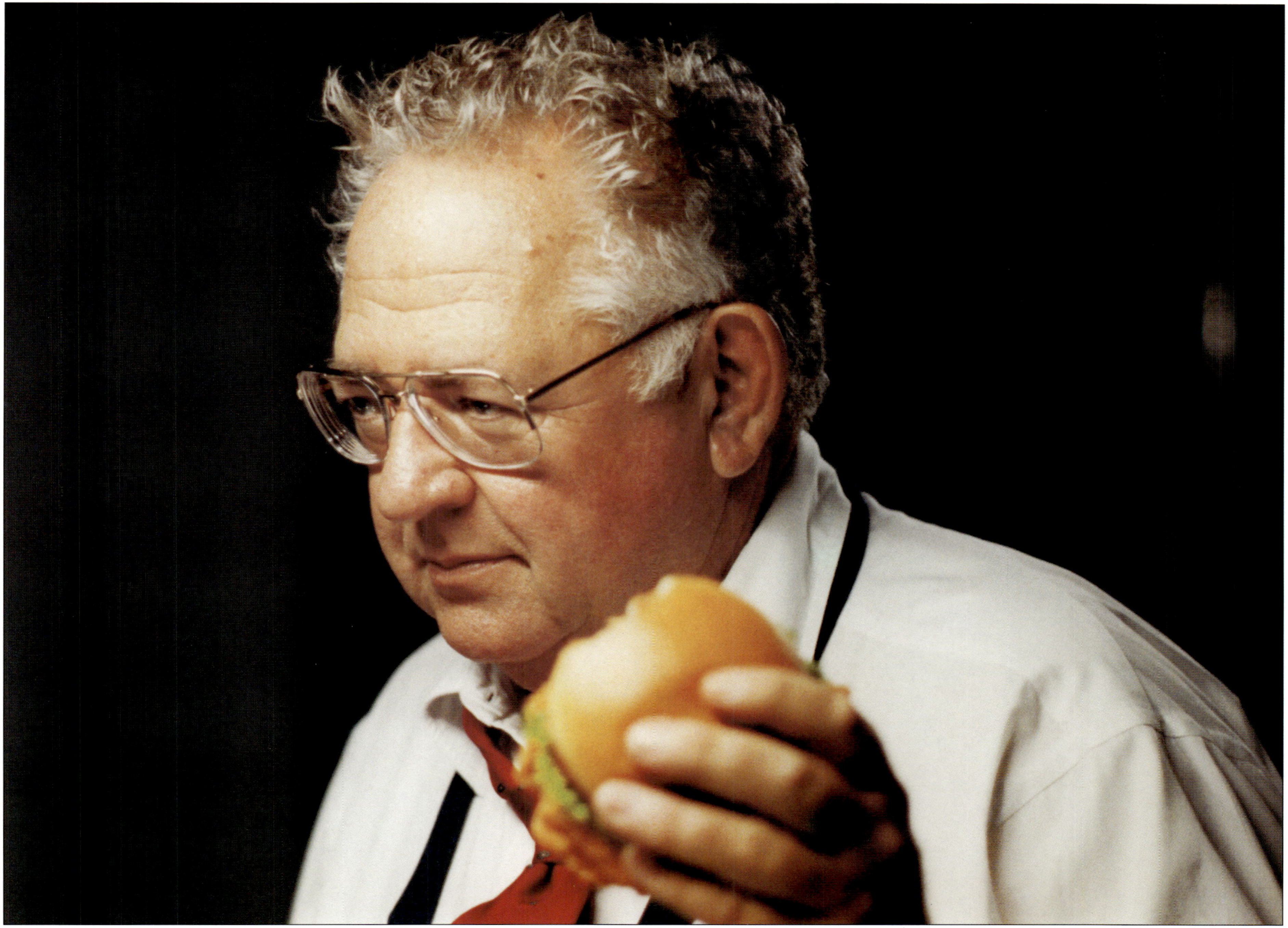

Luckily, there was a Wendy's nearby.

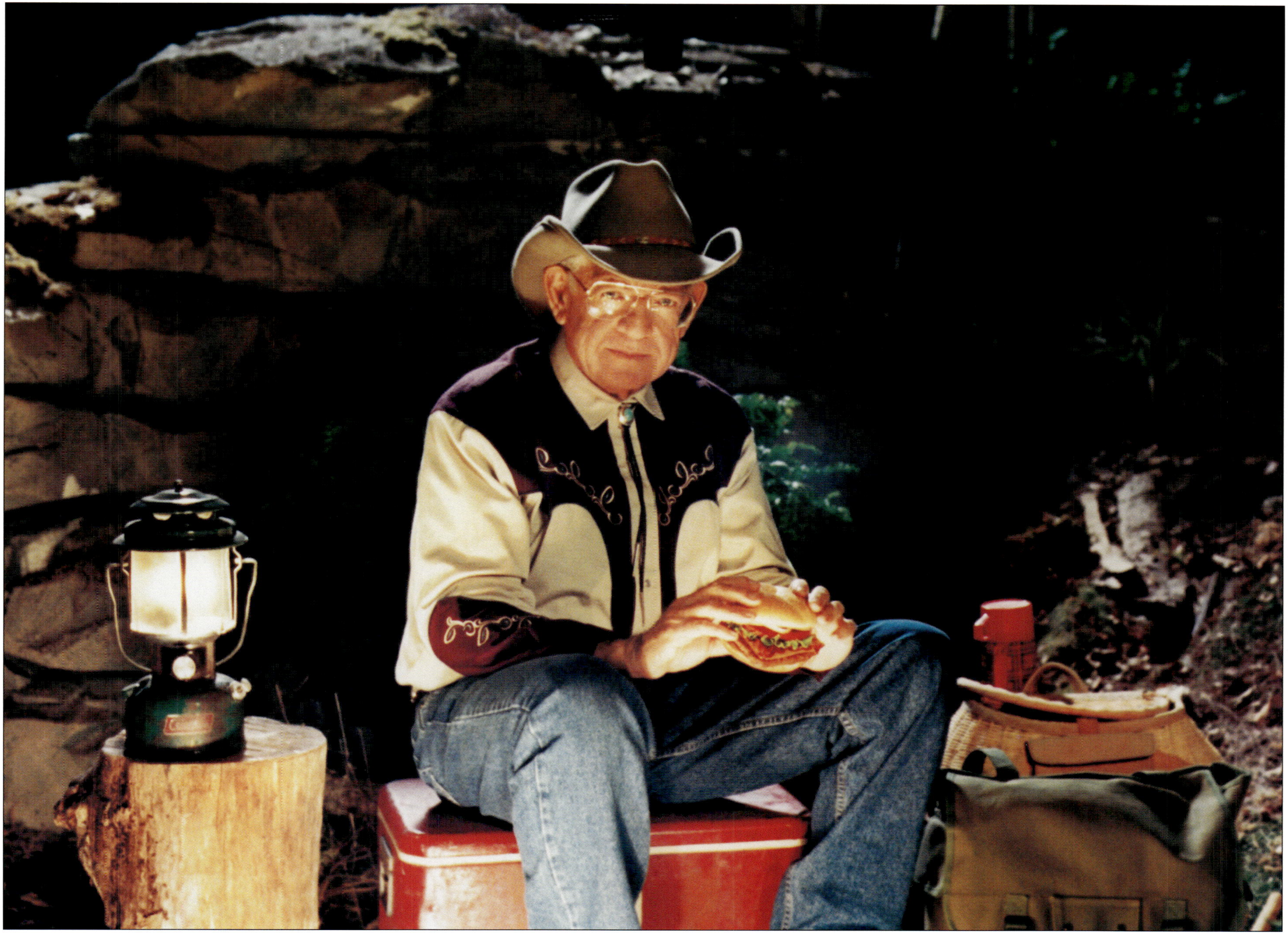

Dave likes hats.

LOTS of hats.

Bonjour!

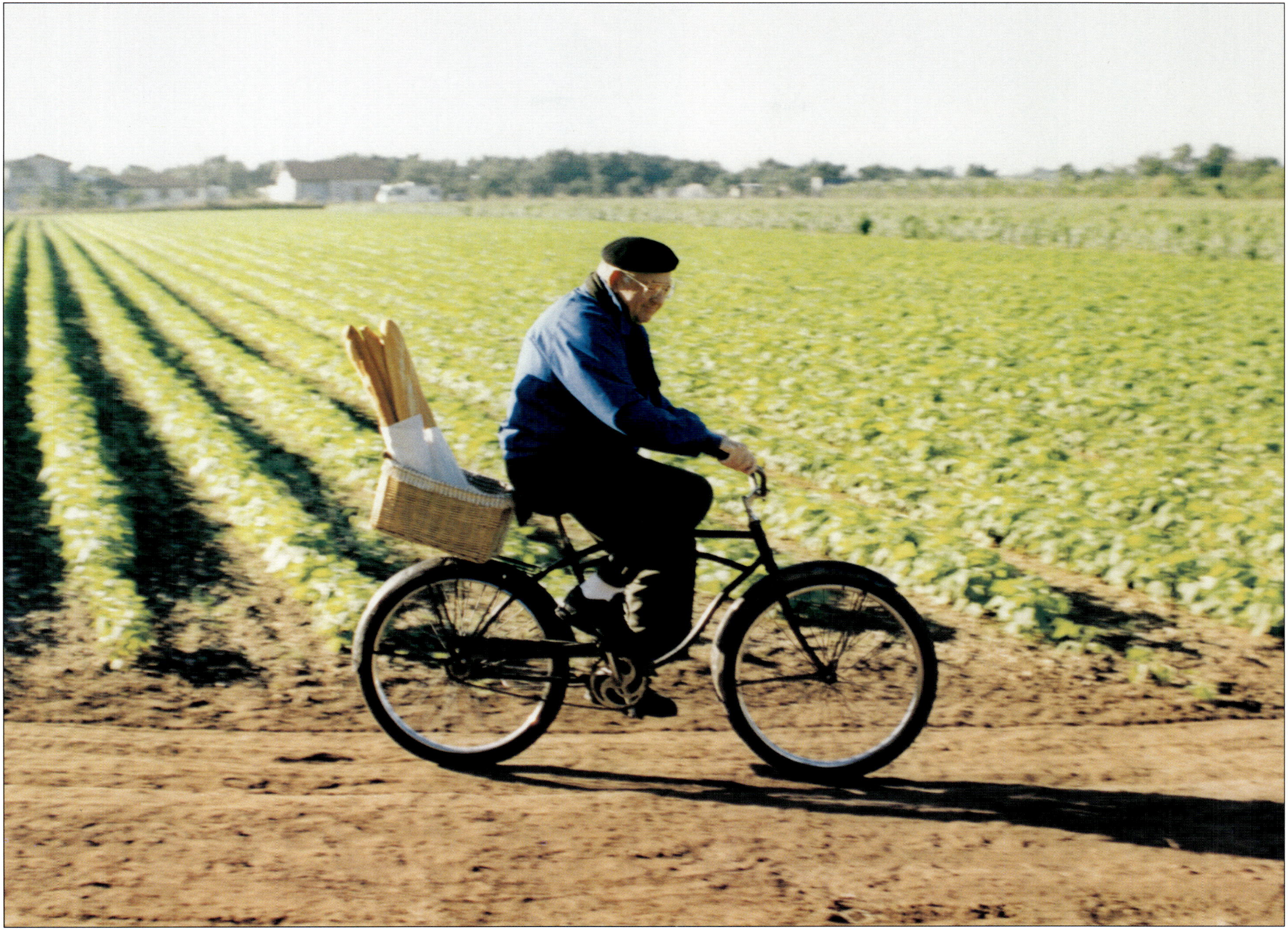

"I'm not gonna wake him, you wake him."

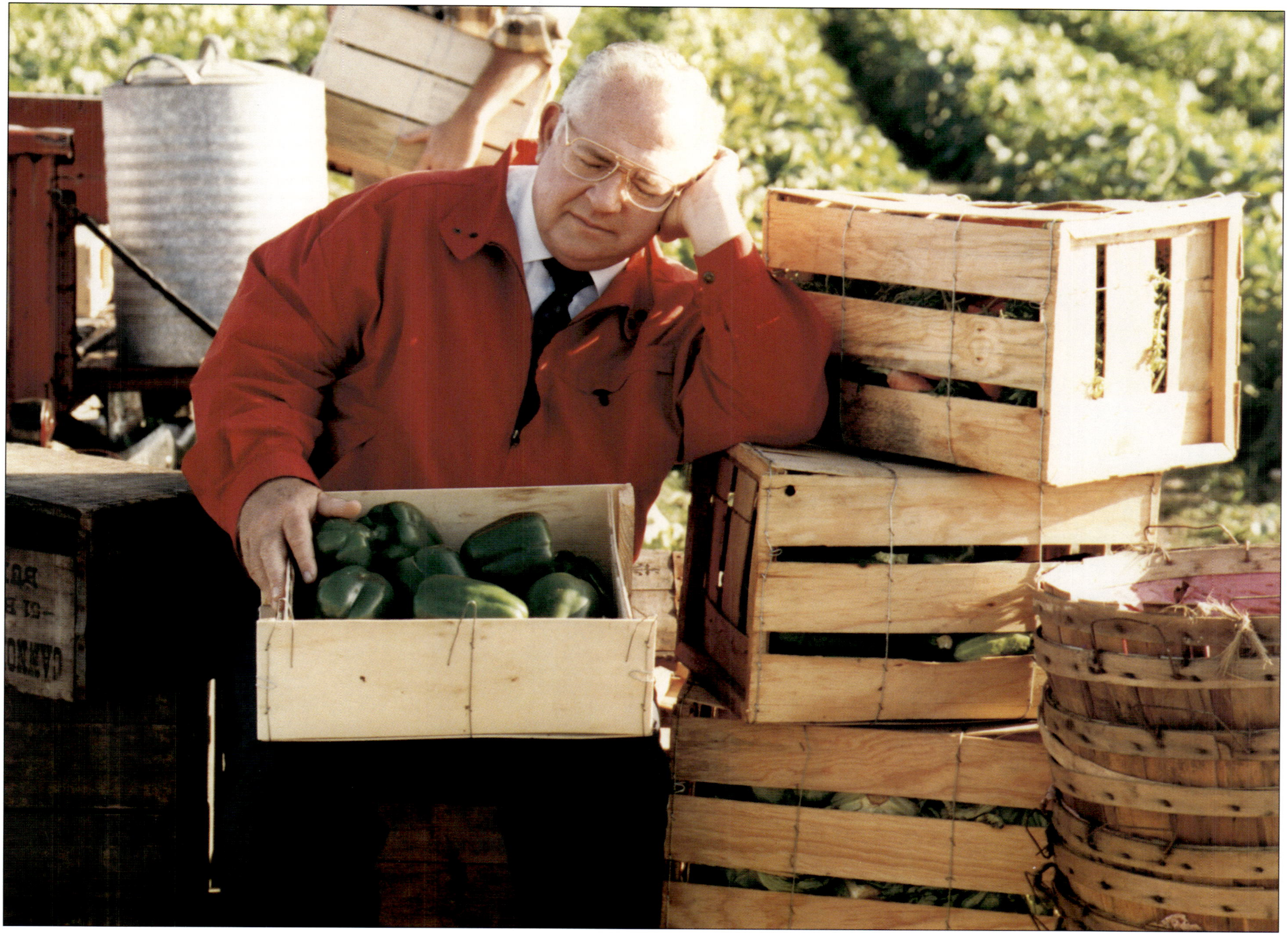

A man of many talents.

Dave juggling before post-production computer magic.

'Did anybody see my marshmallow?'

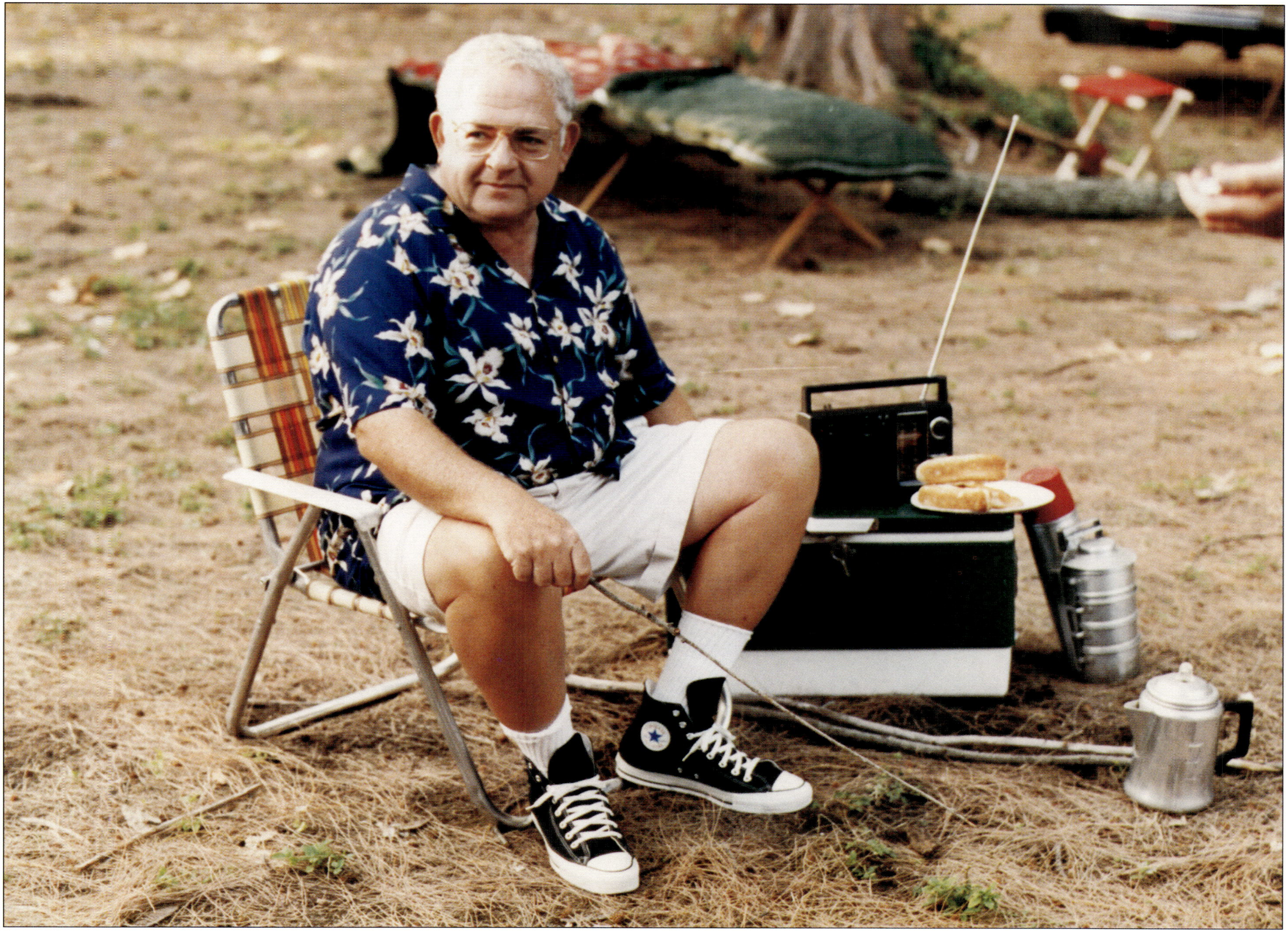

"What hamburger?
I didn't see a hamburger."

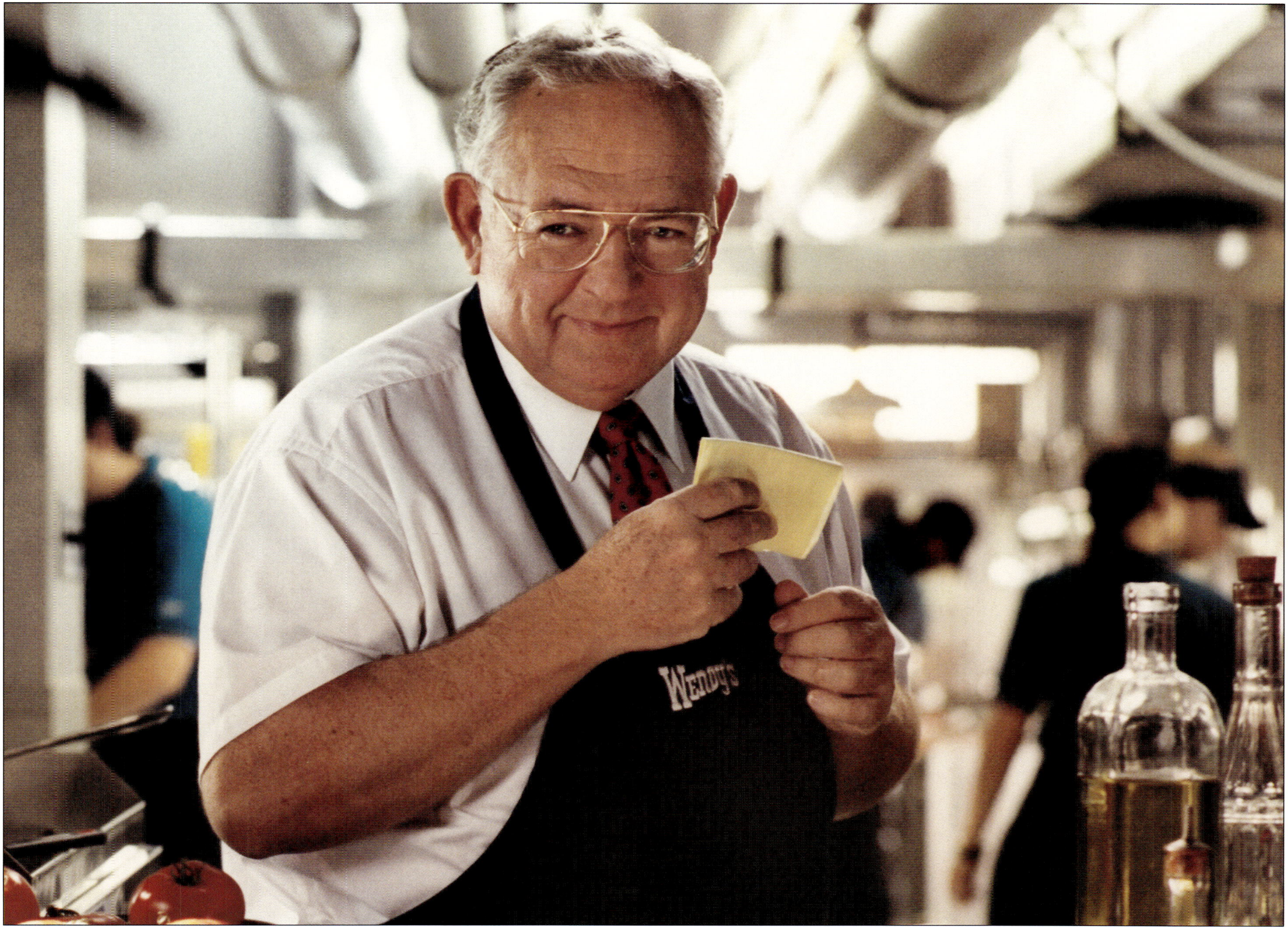
Wendy's

"Is it hot in here, or is it just me?"

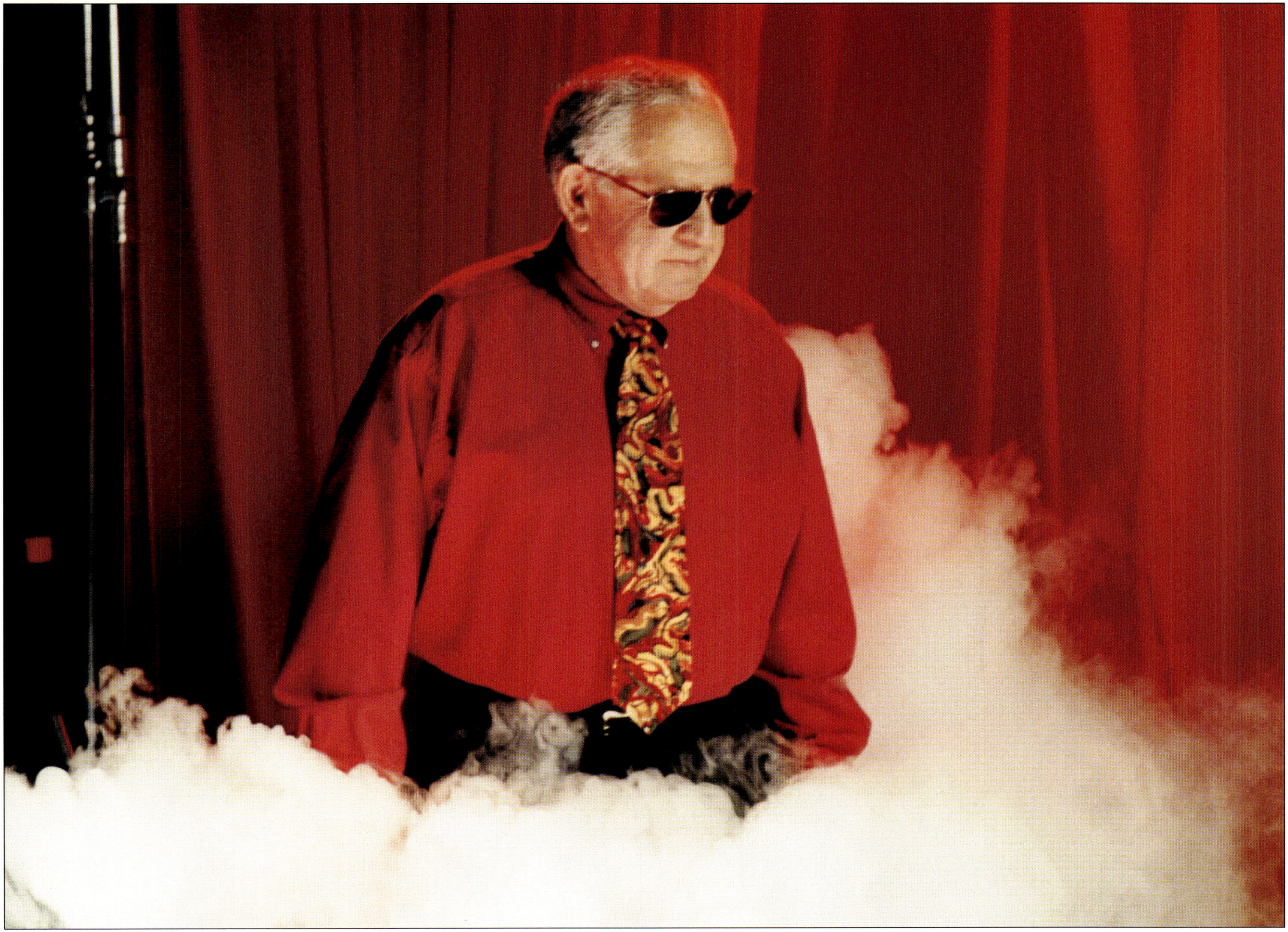

Acting can be a lonely profession.

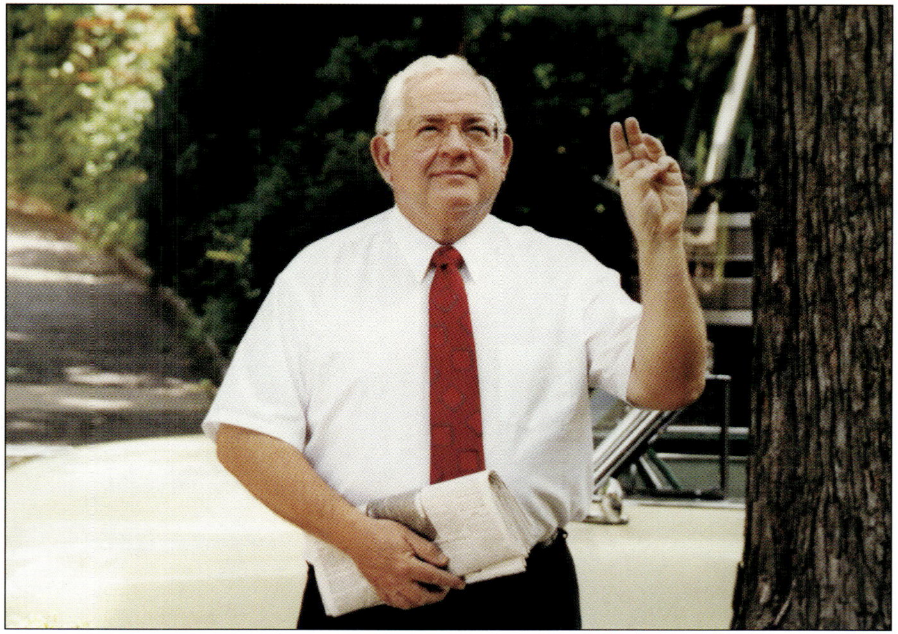

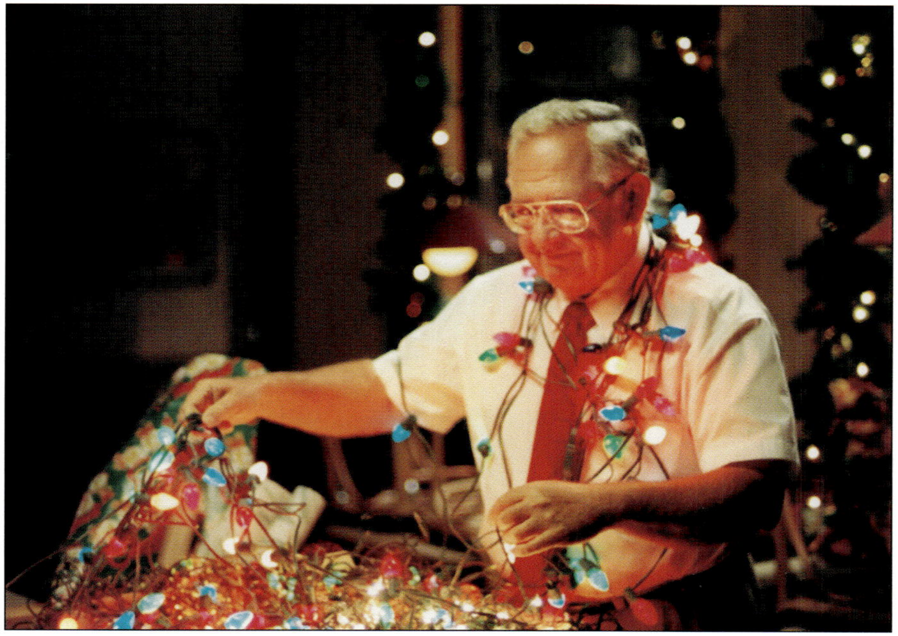

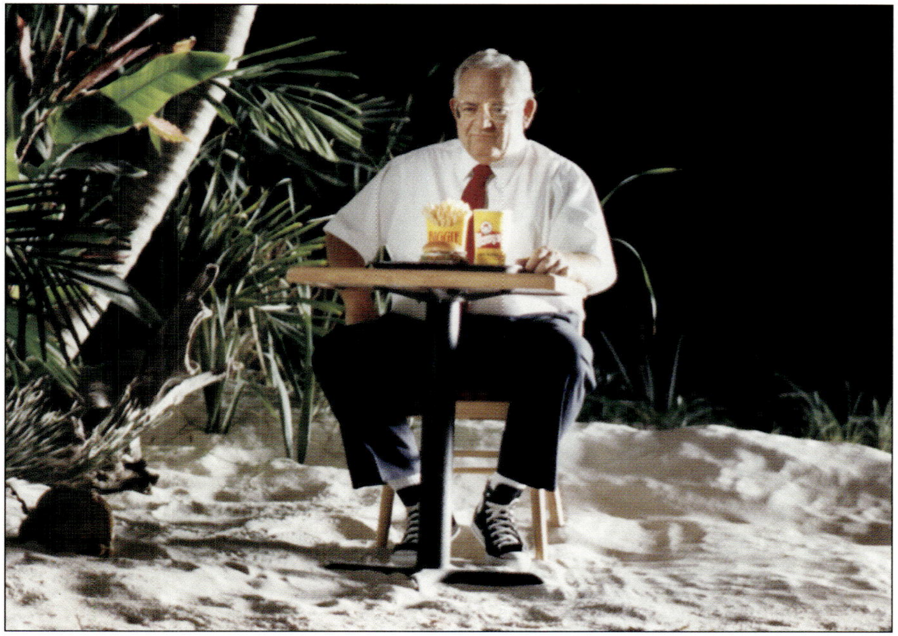

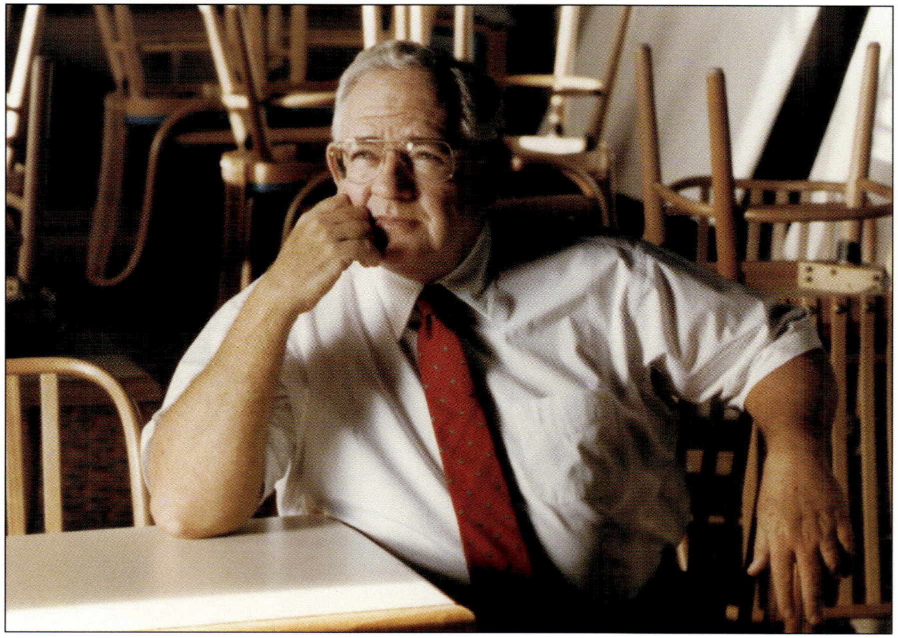

"Sorry Gordon. We're running late.
Can you cover the board meeting?"

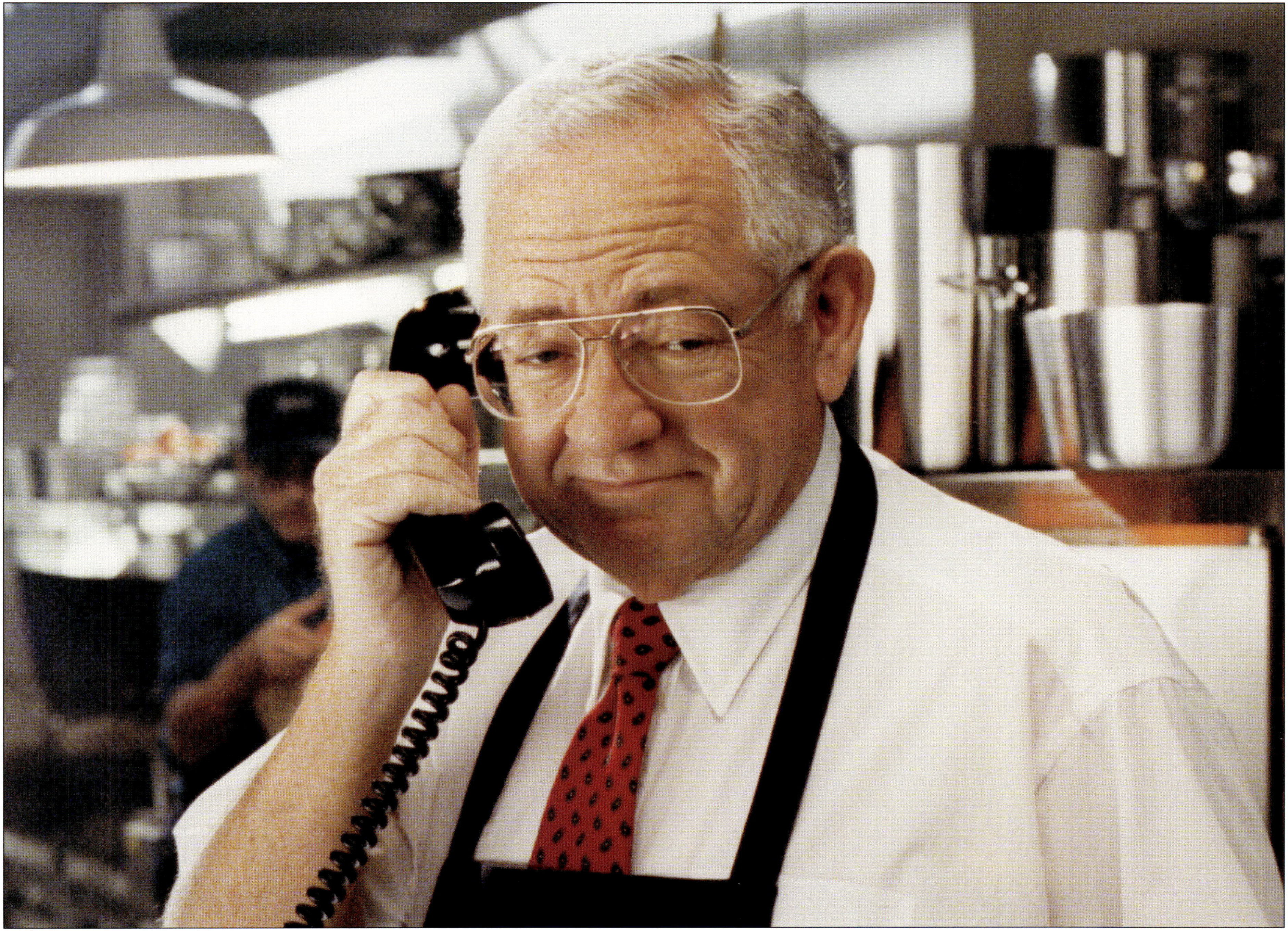

Dave takes a "workbreak" on the set.

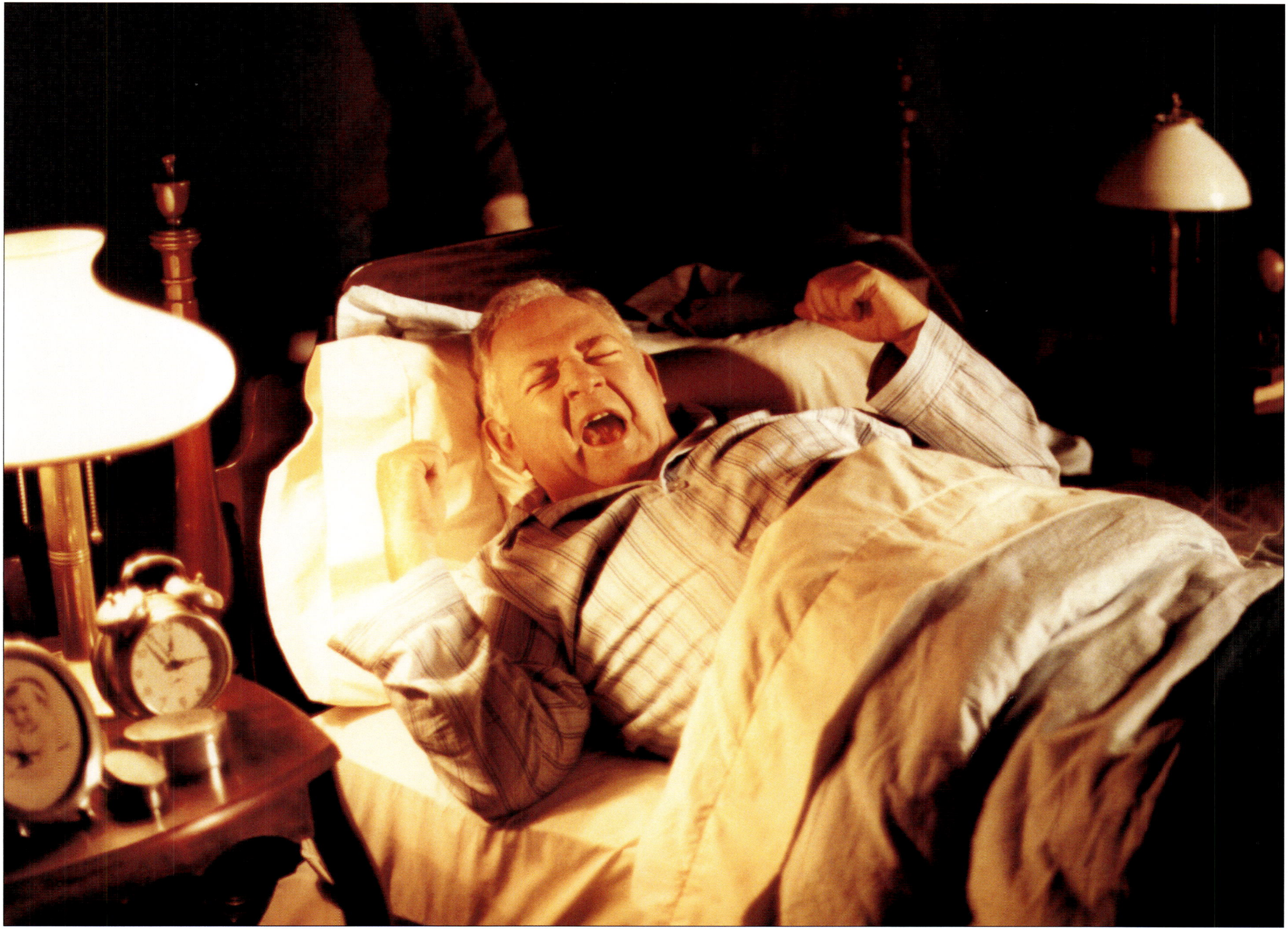

"Tell Mr. Spielberg I'll call him back."

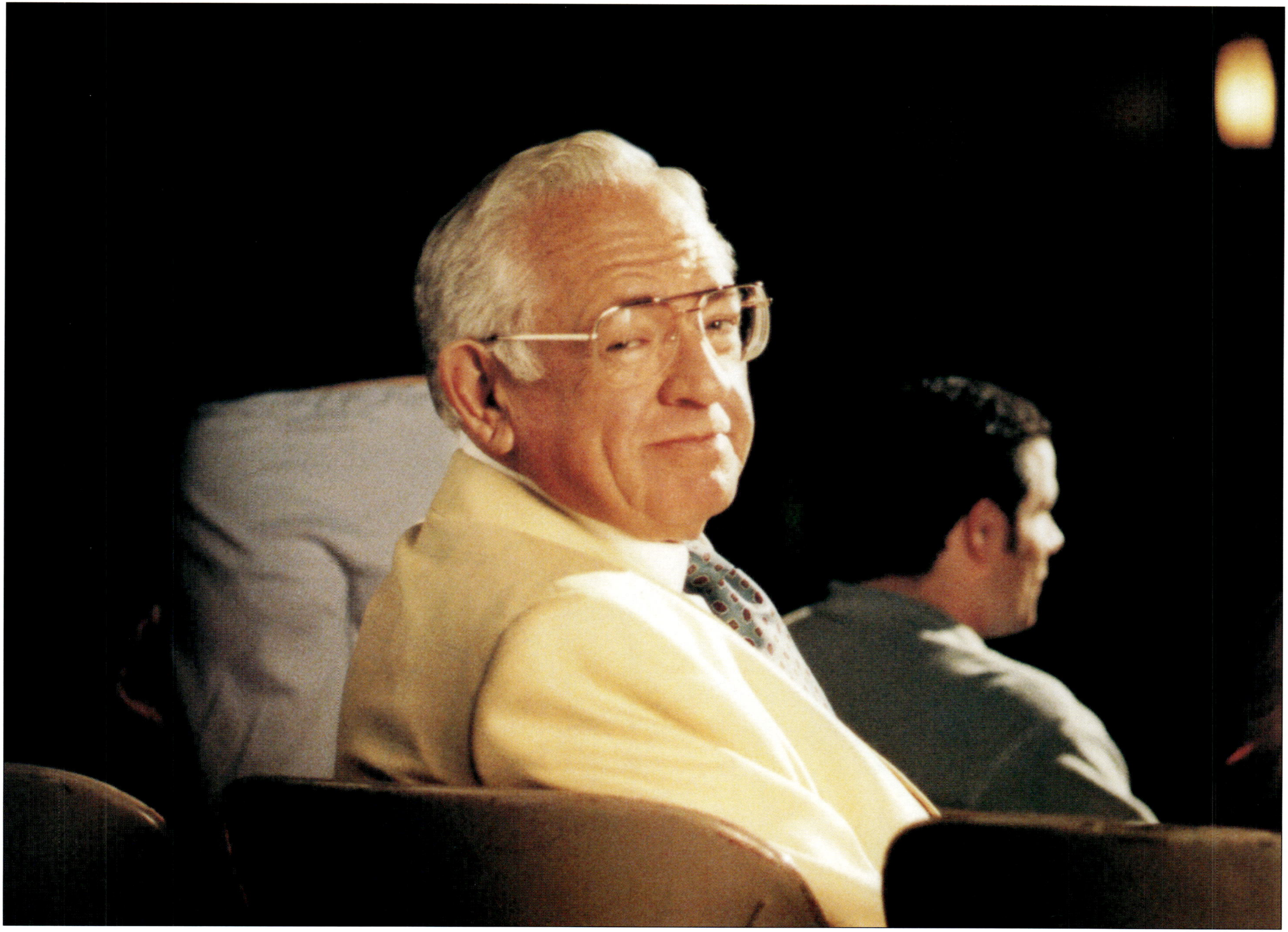

"Perfect."

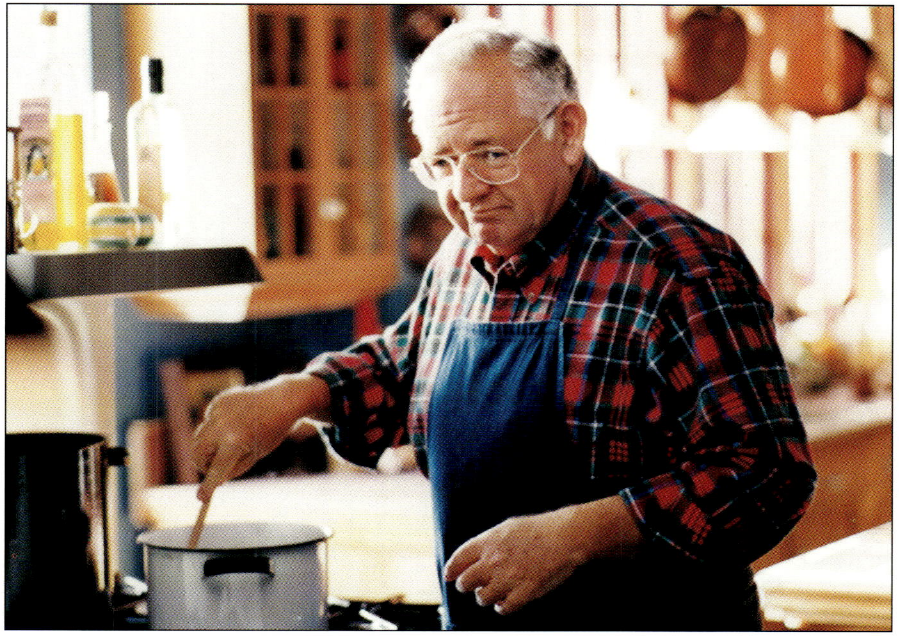
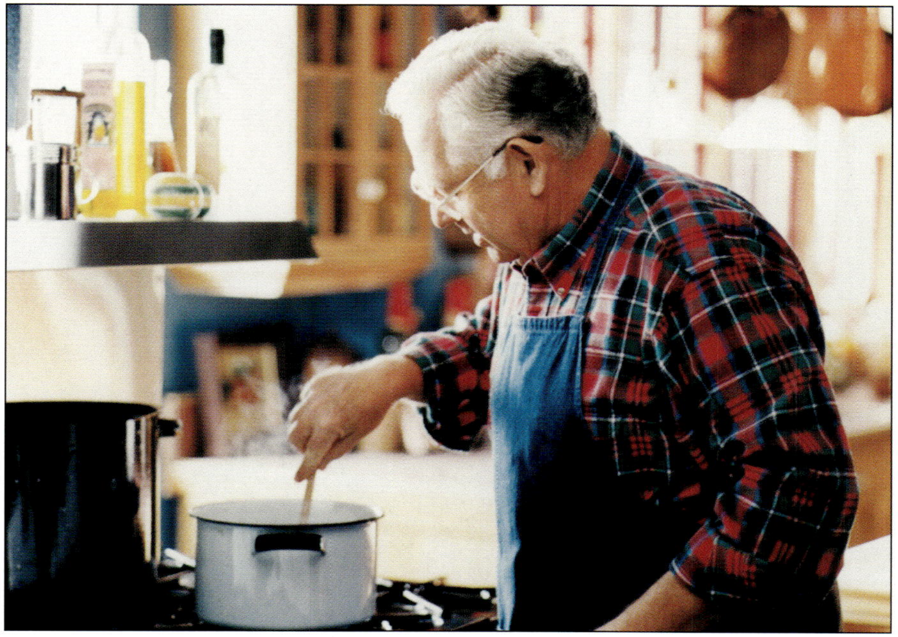
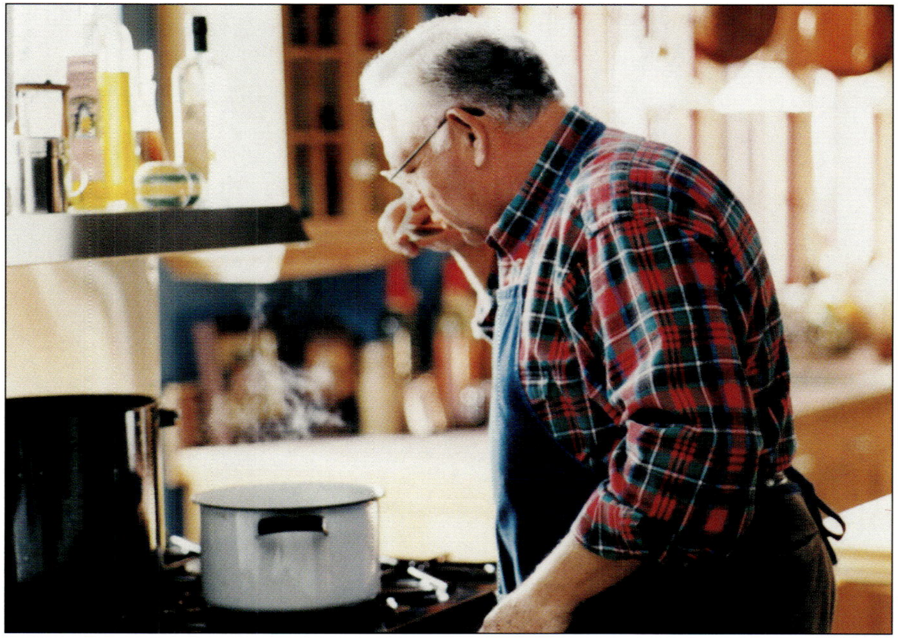
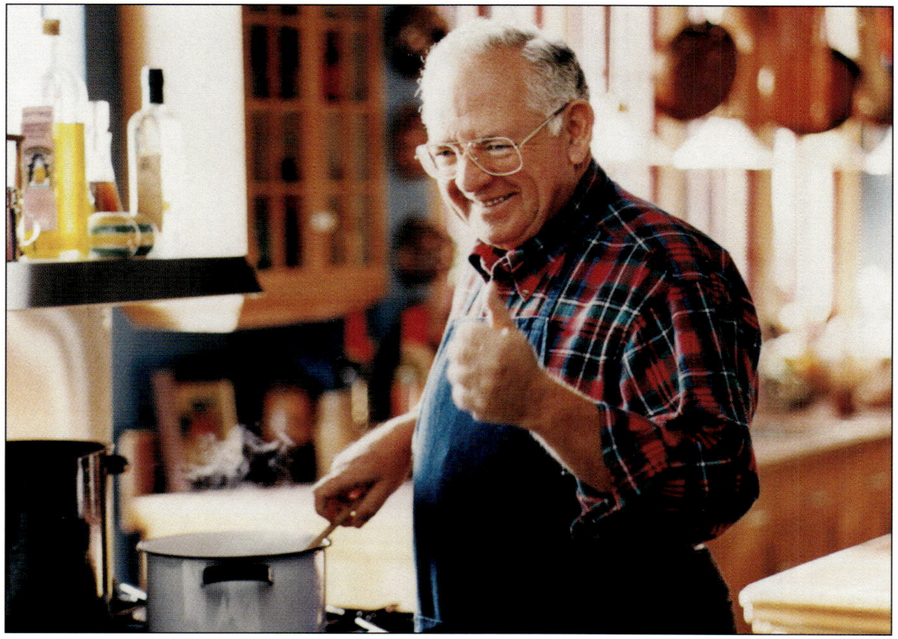

"They did say Tuesday, didn't they?"

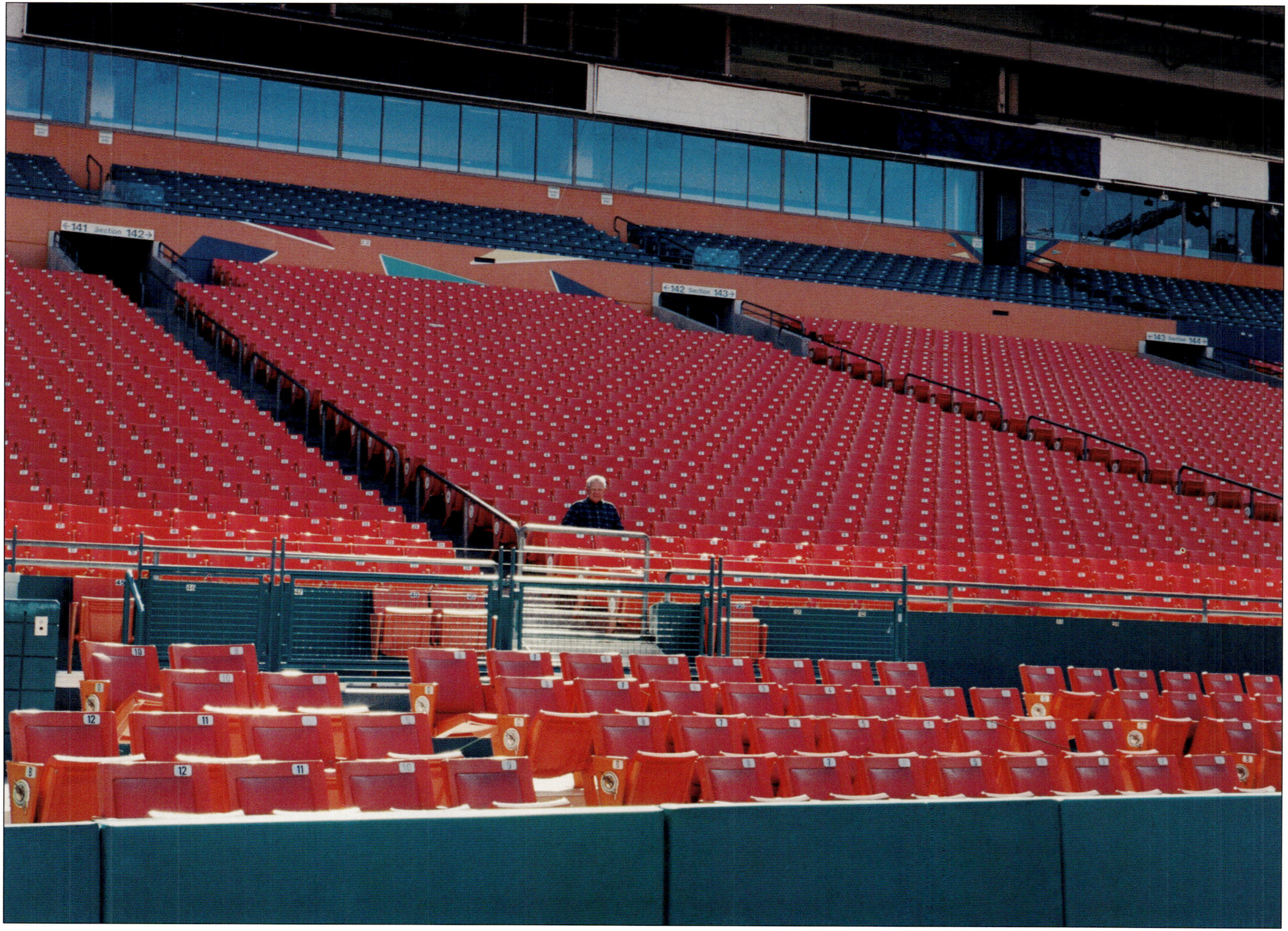
←141 Section 142→
←142 Section 143→
←143 Section 144→

Spicy Chicken brought out Dave's wild side

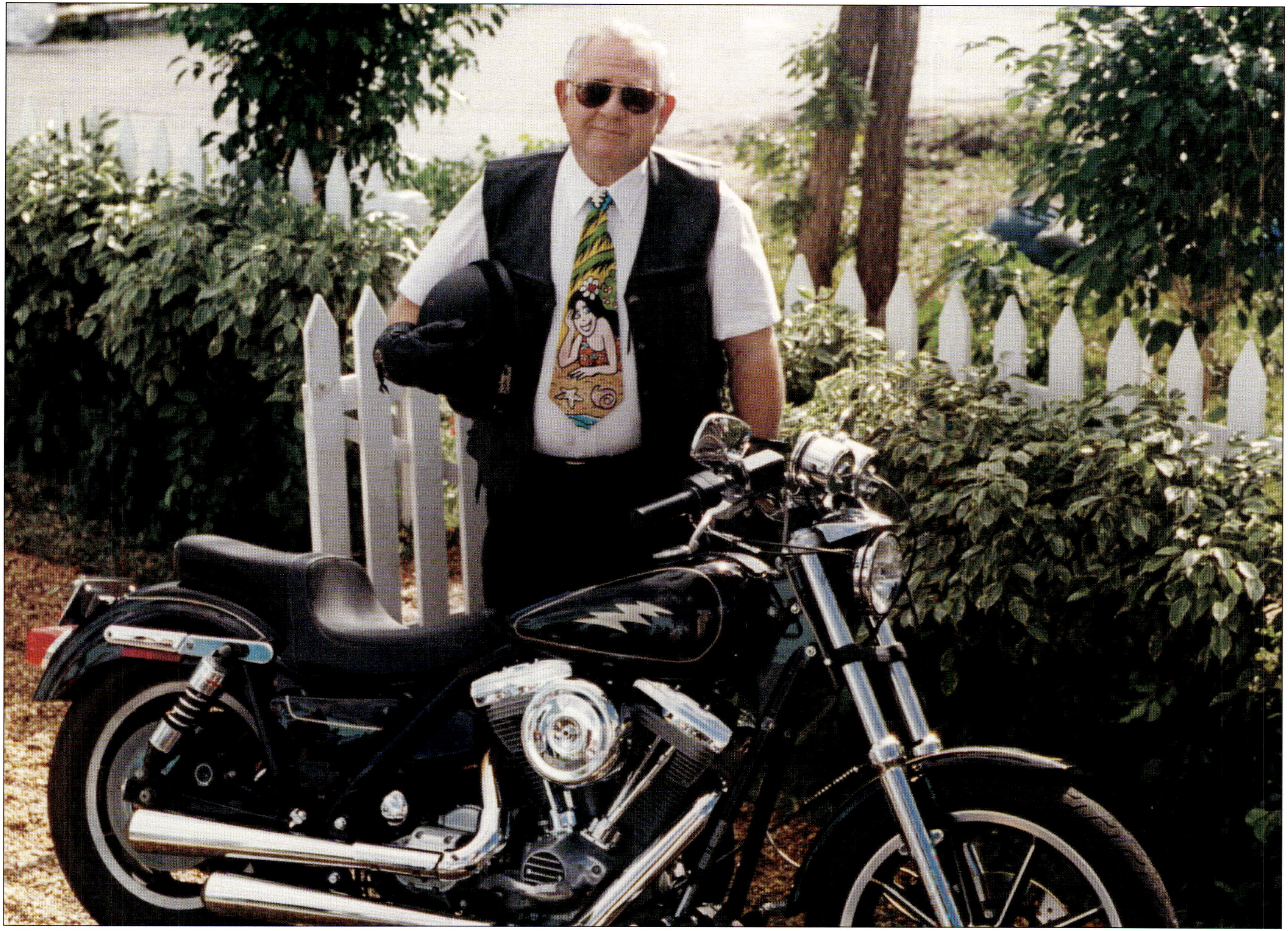

Dave gets caught in a manmade rainstorm.
Luckily, he was able to keep the fries dry.

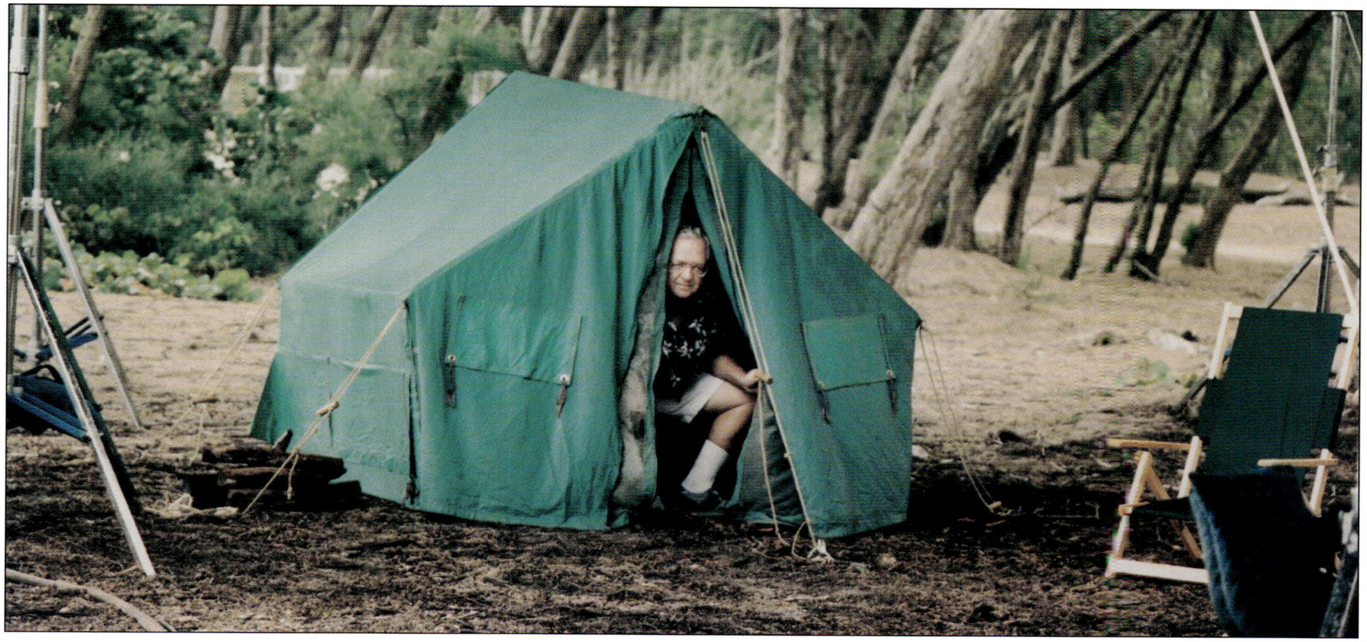

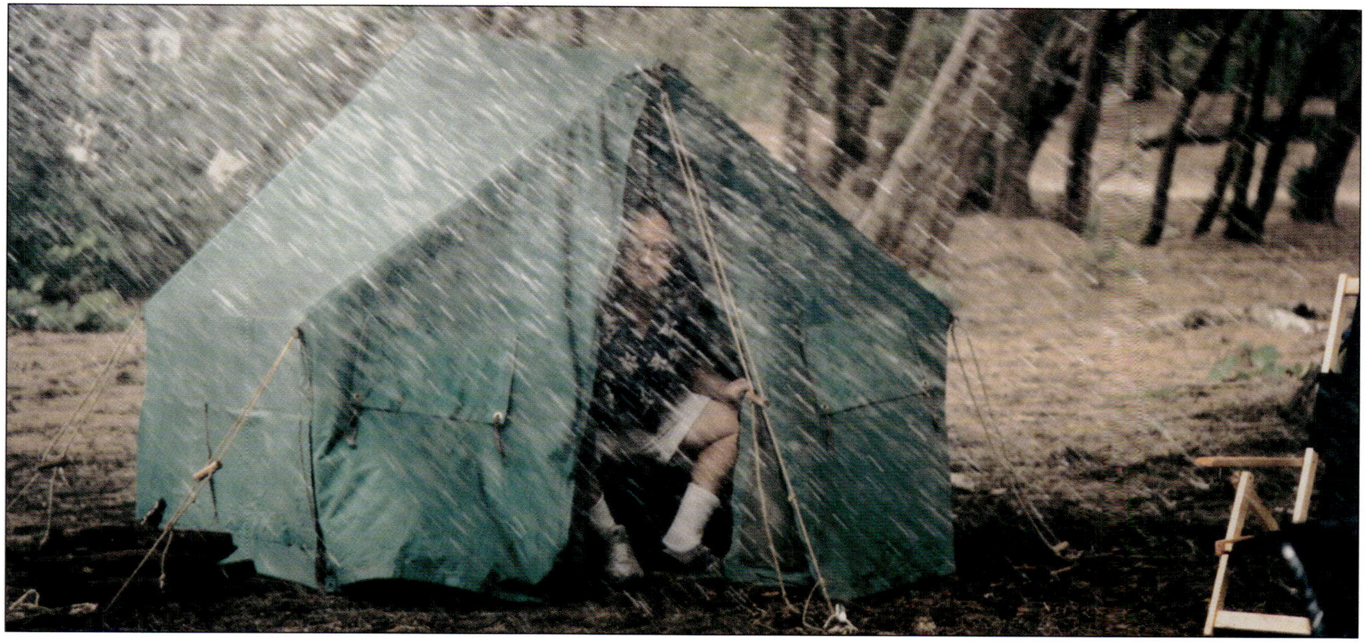

Dave dons many disguises to spread the word about pitas.

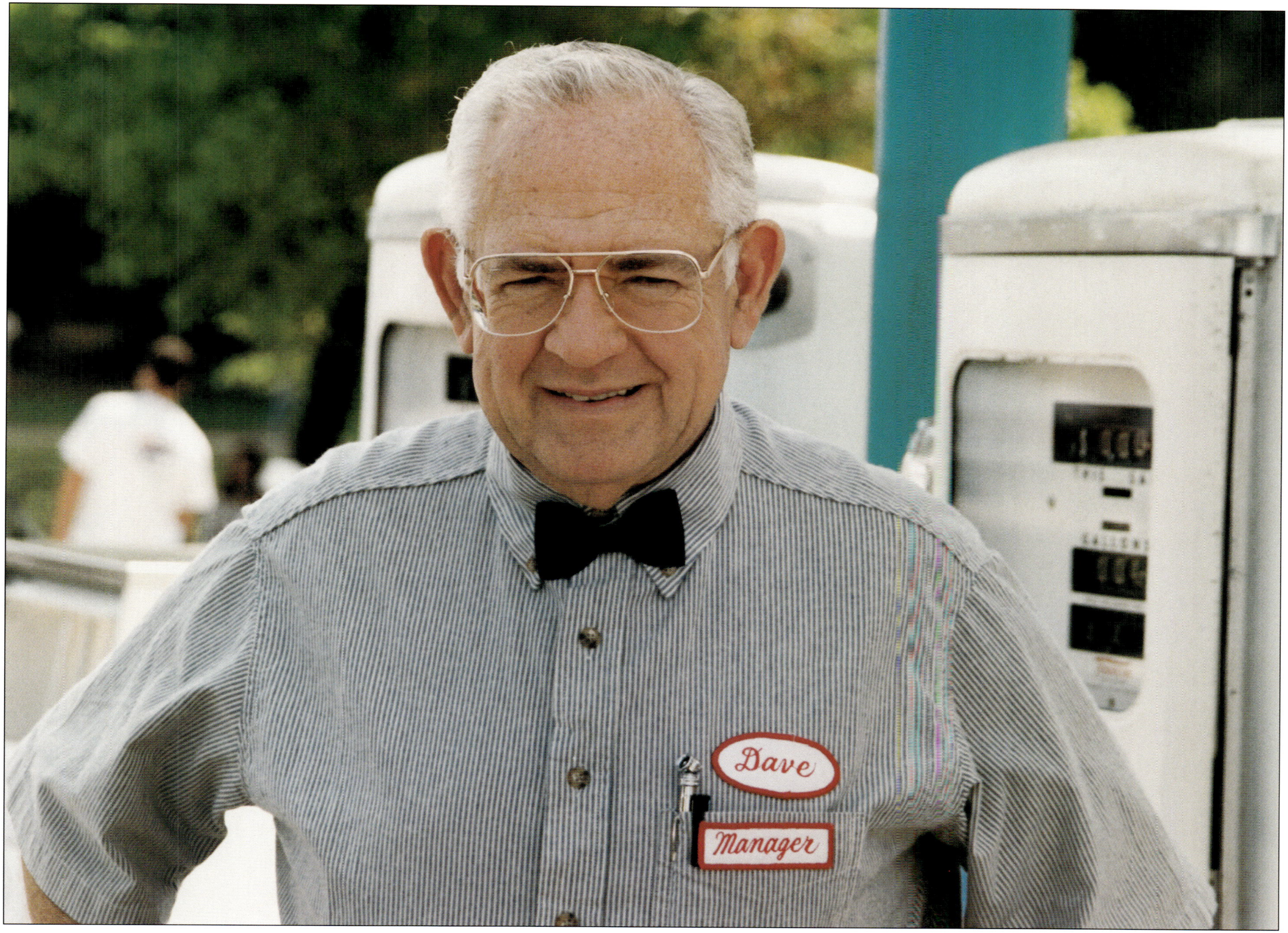
Dave
Manager

"Are you sure this is New Jersey?"

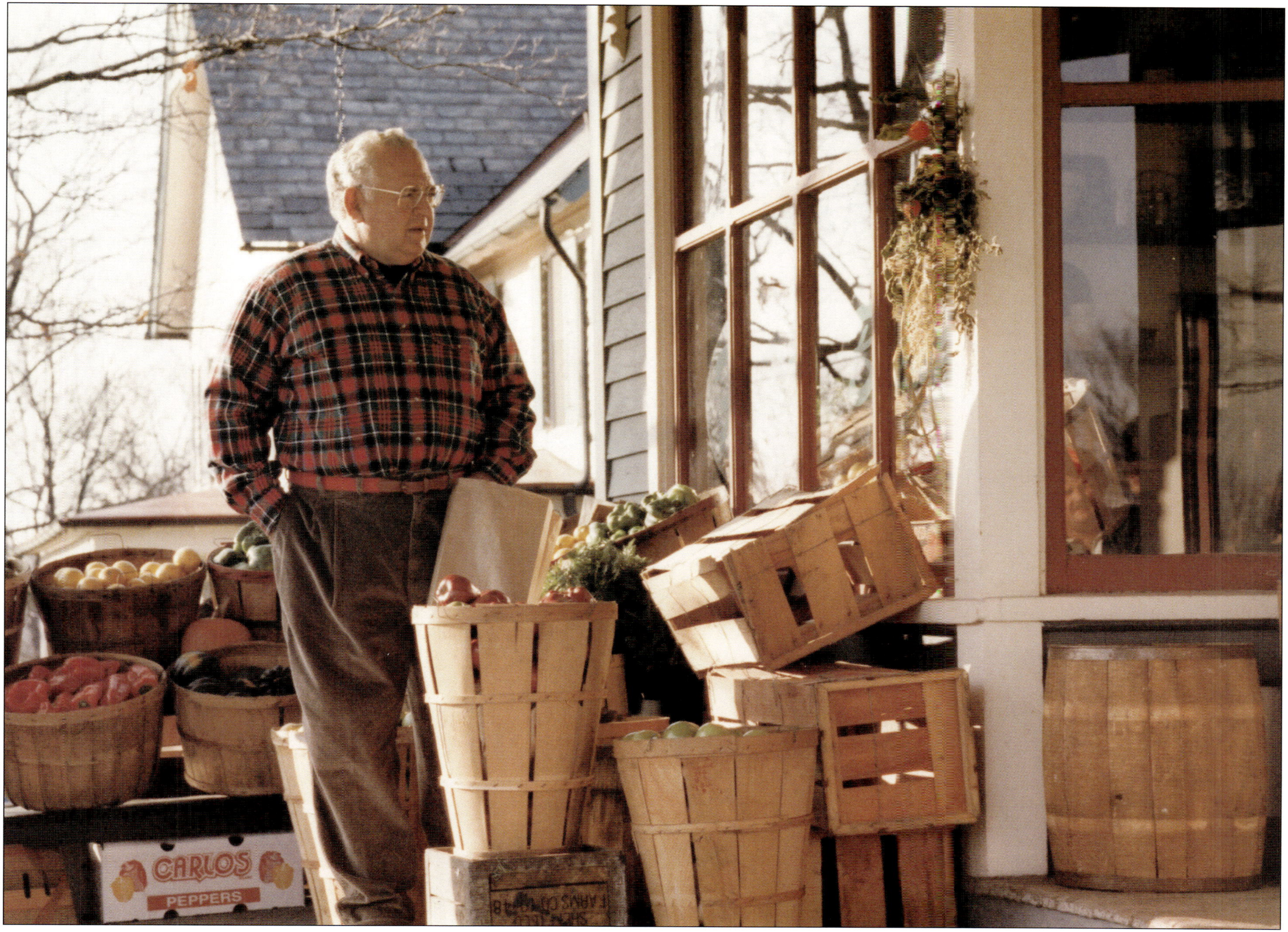
CARLOS
PEPPERS

"I think I used too much water."

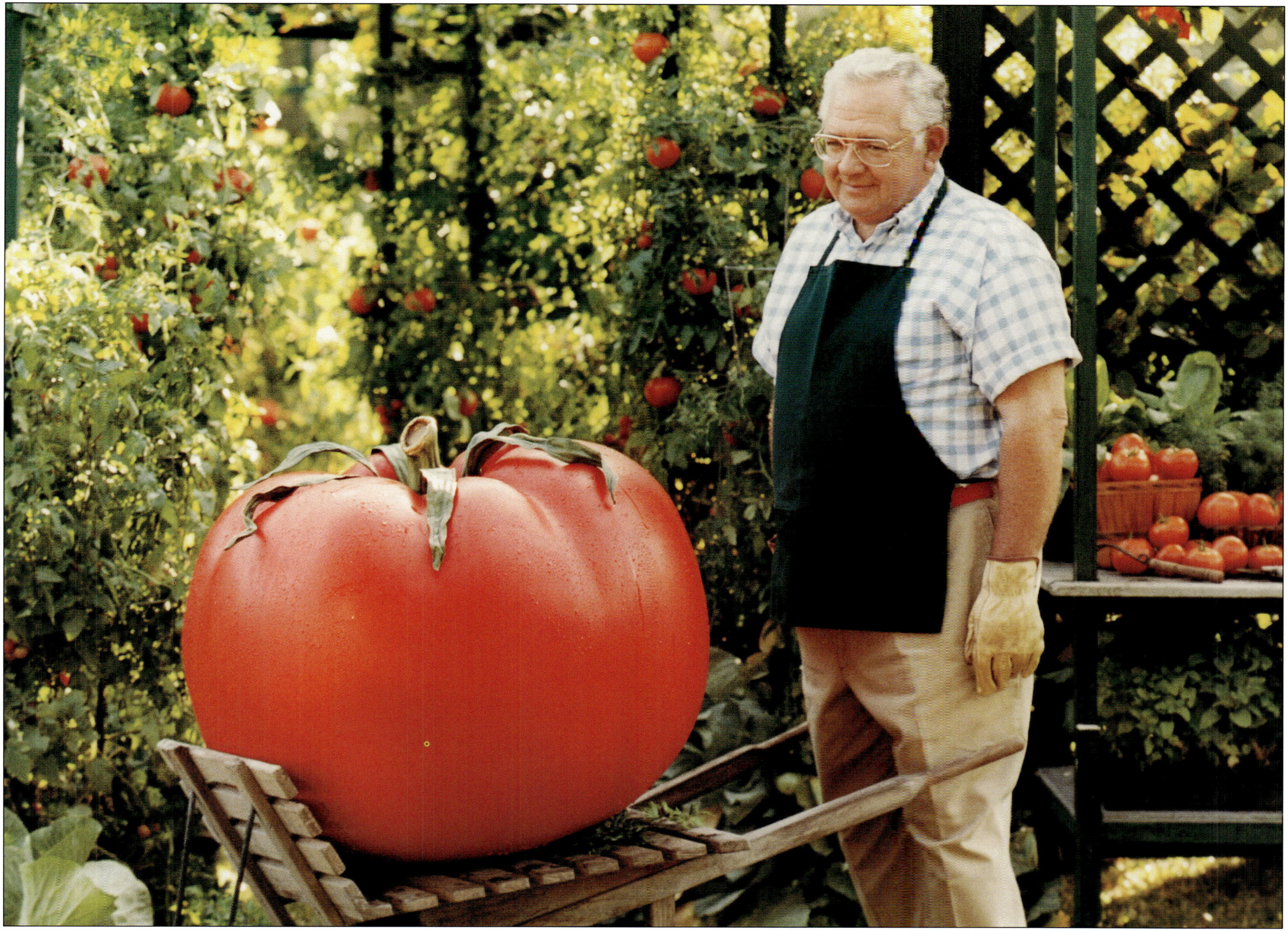

Dave enjoys an indoor walk in the woods
while trying to figure out where the tops of the trees went.

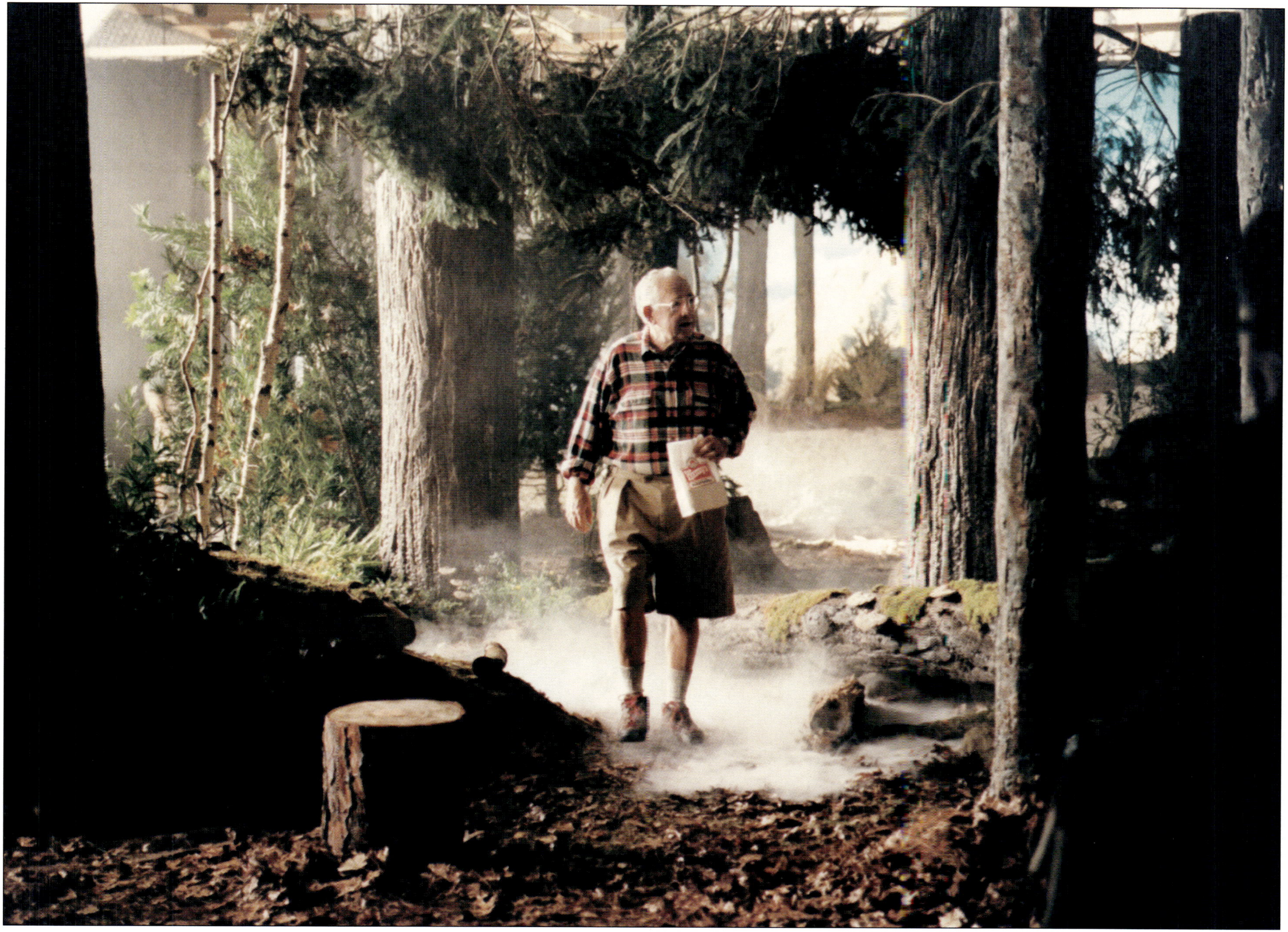

Ten years,
and still going strong.

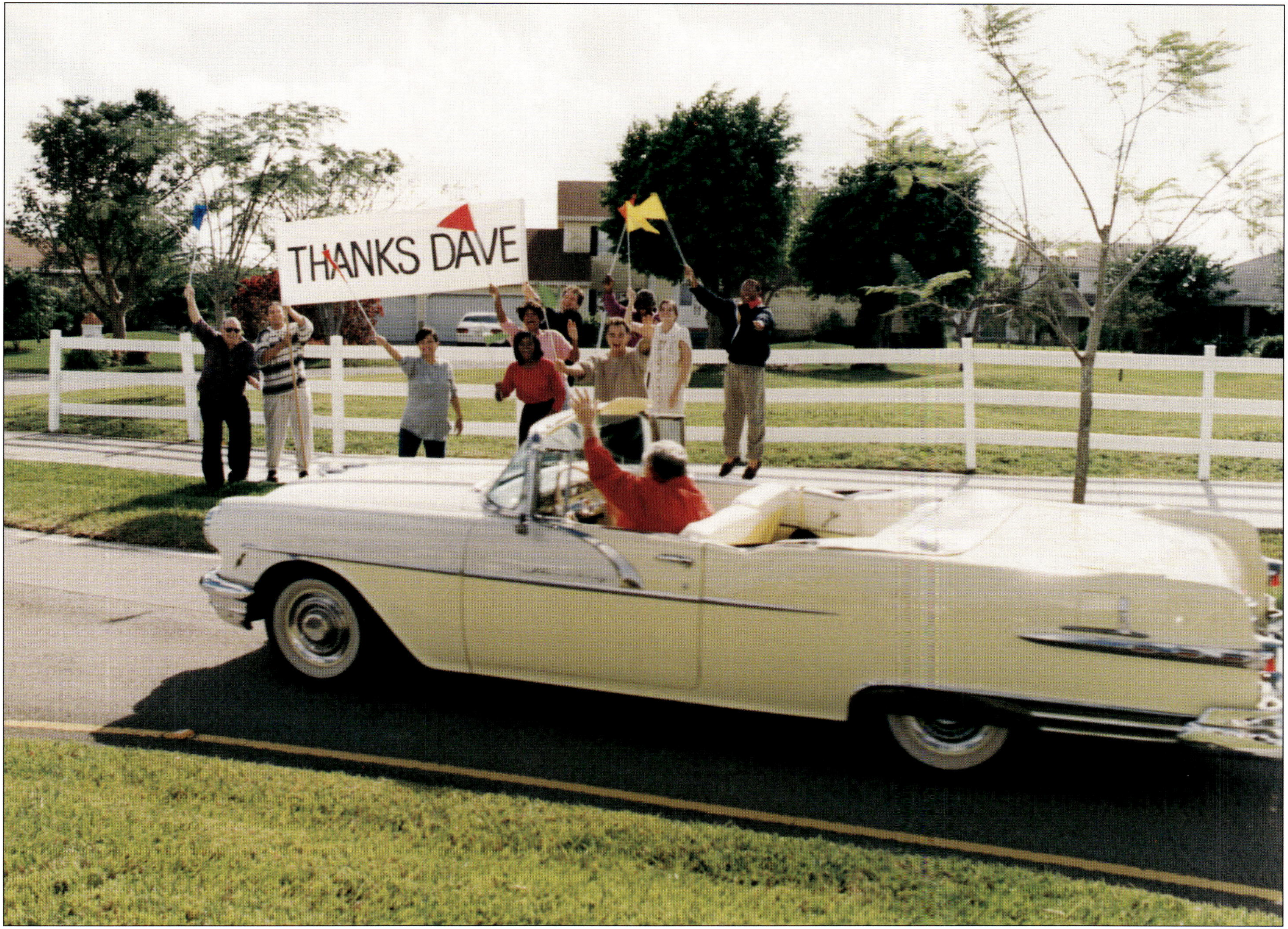
THANKS DAVE

CAST OF CHARACTERS

The following people were involved in all or most of Dave's first 10 years in Advertising. Their talent, vision and hard work has helped make this campaign the success it has become.

WENDY'S
Emil Brolick
Don Calhoon
Matt Dee
Denny Lynch
Jim Near
Charlie Rath
Gordon Teter

BATES USA
Paul Basile
Garry Bergman
Bob Levite
Jim McKennan
Marylin Silverman
Gary Steele
Bailey Weiss

ARTIST COMPANY
Sal Guida
Bill Hudson
Sabrina Palladino

ARF
Alex Fernbach

SLINGSHOT
Marty Ashkinos
Bruce Ashkinos

WNAP
Elliott Arking, Jim Baker, Junior Bridgeman, Michael Cain, Mike Dell'Angelo, Joe Drury, Larry Fleming, Dick Fox, Jim Gill, Bob Goodrich, Jim Hardin, Duane Hoover, David Karam, Ron Kirstien, Mike Kourie, Rob Montgomery, Tom Mulcahy, Dan Nagy, Ron Reinke, John Roberts, Charlie Rodgers, Pete Salg, Columbus Salley, Scott Schmidt, Mike Toukan, Joe Turner, Roger Webb